A COMPLETE GUIDE FOR THE NRI

All that an NRI needs to know about Taxation, Bank Accounts, Investments, Savings & Baggage Rules.

Incorporates The Latest Amendments In The Finance Bill 2007

Sixth Edition

RAGHU PALAT

JAICO PUBLISHING HOUSE

Mumbai Delhi Bangalore Kolkata
Hyderabad Chennai Ahmedabad Bhopal

Published by Jaico Publishing House
121 Mahatma Gandhi Road
Mumbai - 400 001
jaicopub@vsnl.com
www.jaicobooks.com

A COMPLETE GUIDE FOR THE NRI
ISBN 81-7992-348-7

Sixth Updated Edition: 2007

Printed by
New Radharaman Printers
20, Wadala Udyog Bhavan
Wadala, Mumbai-400 031

TO

MY FAMILY AND MY FRIENDS

RAGHU PALAT
A BIOGRAPHICAL SKETCH

Raghu Palat is one of India's leading writers on banking, finance and investments. He has authored twenty- five extremely well received books.

Raghu Palat is the great grandson of His Highness, Rama Varma the Maharaja of Cochin, and of Sir Chettur Sankaran Nair who was a member of the Viceroy's Executive Council and a former President of the Indian National Congress. Mr. Palat is, by profession, a banking consultant. Mr. Palat has been instrumental in the restructuring of banks and in developing strategies for banks in India and abroad. He has earlier held very senior-level executive positions with multinational banks in India and abroad. He is also a director in Cheque Mate Infotech Private Ltd., a company that manages a finance portal called *www.bankingrules.com* He conducts workshops on Effective Business Writing, Business Etiquette, Effective Presentation Skills, Banking and Finance.

Mr. Palat is an acknowledged authority on banking, investment, and finance. He is a Fellow of the Institute of Chartered Accountants in England and Wales, and an Associate of the Institute of Chartered Accountants of India. He has lectured as a visiting faculty member at the invitation of the Bankers Training College, Mumbai, and the South East AsiaCentral Bankers Association (SEACEN), which is headquartered in Malaysia.

Raghu Palat lives in Mumbai with his family consisting of his wife Pushpa, two daughters, Divya and Nikhila, son in law Aditya and their cocker spaniels, Champ and Cookie.

OTHER BOOKS BY THE AUTHOR

FICTION

- Anguish

NON-FICTION

- Tax Planning for the Salaried Employee
- The Credit Report
- The Magic of Ratios
- The Wonderworld of Investments
- Understanding Ratios
- How to Read Annual Reports and Balance Sheets
- Investments – Where and When
- Understanding Financial Ratios in Business
- Shares for Investment and Wealth
- Fundamental Analysis of Shares
- Documentary Letters of Credit and Collections
- How to apply for a Bank Loan and get it sanctioned
- How to manage Foreign Exchange Risks
- Effective Business Writing
- Interview Tips – Get the job you want.
- Everything an Indian needs to know on Business Etiquette
- Secrets of their Success – Achievers from the World of Finance
- Corporate leaders – Secrets of their success
- Retail Banking – Everything you need to know to work in a bank
- Self Made High achievers – Secrets of their success
- The Bank of India Story
- Banking Fundamentals
- The Negotiable Instruments Act
- Retail Banking

DISCLAIMER

The opinions expressed in this book are those of the author and must not be construed as the opinion of any other person, company or institution. Any resemblance to any person, company or institution is purely coincidental.

The author has, as far as possible, attempted to provide up-to-date information on the various matters that have been written in the book. However, in case of doubt, readers are advised to either refer to official publications or their own advisers (especially where there is an issue of interpretation). Readers should remember that these are times when India is liberalizing many archaic rules. Therefore, prior to taking a decision, it is advisable to check what the current regulation is.

This book is sold with the clear understanding that neither the author, the publishers, the promoters, the resellers nor anyone else involved in any way with this book are not responsible or liable for the result of an action taken (based on a suggestion made in this book) by the reader or for any error or omission.

CONTENTS

ACKNOWLEDGMENTS

I returned to India in 1978 after nine years abroad. To understand the business environment, economic situation and taxation, I devoured several professional magazines, business papers, tax books, law books and other technical tomes. Apart from being heavy and cumbersome, they made hard reading. And these tomes were also very trying and boring. In frustration, I often complained to my wife, Pushpa and ventured comments on how the articles should have been written and what should have been included. In exasperation after being months of being at the receiving end of criticism and complaints, she said, "If you are so critical and know so much, why don't you write?" The gauntlet was thrown. With some apprehension, I picked it up. I wrote. I rewrote. Pushpa, with infinite patience, commented and criticized. I wrote again. This process of review and revision continued till it passed the acid test – Pushpa's approval. Having written it, what next? Someone has to publish it. Pushpa once again helped me. She suggested that I take it to the most widely read business newspaper in Mumbai, which, at that time, was the Economic Times. Clutching my precious article, I went to its spartan office. A gentleman there, a Mr. Mathews, on ascertaining the reason for my presence, much to my chagrin, indifferently dropped my precious treasure into a tray. I left. Great was our delight when ten days later, the article was published as an editorial. Thus began my romance with writing. And, in all my writing, I have tried to faithfully adhere to the reason that set me on this path – the article, book or report must be such that the reader must be able to understand it easily. I, once again, thank Pushpa, my wife and best friend for challenging me to write and for supporting and encouraging me always.

This book would not have been written had it not been for the persistent efforts of the affable Mr. Rayasam Sharma, the Editor of Jaico – a marketing man par excellence, a terrific editor and above all, a wonderful human being. He first broached this subject to me in the spring of 1998. Then, relentlessly, at every meeting and with emails, he pursued me till I consented. This book is the result. Thank you, Mr. Sharma, for being so tenacious. Had it not been for your persistence, this book would not have seen the light of day. And I would never have known so much about the rules and regulations pertaining to Non-Resident Indians.

I want to acknowledge and thank several of my non-resident friends – for their thoughts, their confusion and their ideas. In particular, I would like to acknowledge my brother Dr. Ravi Palat (of the world – I use this word advisedly as one is usually unsure where he is at any time).

I would like to acknowledge all those who had faith in my writing and encouraged me over the years – the editors of the Economic Times, The Financial Express, Business Update, Business World, Mid Day, Fortune, The Sunday Observer, The Independent, The Times of India and other newspapers and magazines that have supported me and published my works. Special thanks to Ayaz Memon, now with DNA who had been the editor of both the Bombay Times and the Mid Day,S and R. Jagannathan now with the DNA but earlier with Business Standard, Myiris.com, Business World, Business Today and the Financial Express. Their vision, their joie de vivre, vitality and drive have always challenged me to seek greater heights.

I am also grateful to the publishers of my books who have supported me – Ashwin Shah, Akash Shah and Rayasam Sharma of Jaico, Harkin Chatlani and Kamal Jagwani of India Book

Distributors, and Kapil Malholtra of Vision Books.

I am grateful to the readers of my columns and my books. It is for them that I write. Thank you for your support.

I must acknowledge my father, Sankaran Palat. He believed in me and it was he who told me that I could write. He encouraged me to write a book when I was only 18. I am so sorry that he is not here to see and read the books I have written.

I thank my two lovely daughters, Nikhila and Divya, for their support, patience and love. I am conscious too of the other two members of my family – Champ and Cookie. Many a time, they sat and kept vigil by me while the rest of the world slept.

PREFACE

The last year has been unprecedented in Indian History. In 2006 and 2007, we have seen Indians foray into new markets in a bid to capture world markets – Mittal and Arcelor, Tata and Corus, Mahindra and Mahindra, Videocon – the list is numerous. I remember many years ago when I was in New York, someone mentioned that New Yorkers get terribly upset when Japanese take a photograph of a building as they suspect that they may buy it. This is now true of Indians venturing abroad. The question no longer is how much but what next? I am heartened. This is a great time to be an Indian.

With a GDP growth rate of 9.2% in 2006, the Indian economy is among the fastest growing in the world. It has the world's third largest GDP of US $4.042 trillion as measured by purchasing power parity (PPP). India's per capita income (PPP) of US $3,700 is however ranked 117th in the world. When measured in terms of the USD exchange-rate, India's GDP is US$785.47 billion, which makes it the twelfth - largest economy.

India's fortunes have changed dramatically. However, since 1991, India has gradually opened up its markets through economic exchange reserves have risen from US$5.8 billion in March 1991 (barely three weeks imports) to US$195 billion in early March 2007, while federal and state budget deficits have reduced. Moreover privatisation of publicly-owned companies and the opening of certain sectors to private and foreign participation have continued amid political debate. The focus has changed. As opposed to attracting dollars, the questions posed now are:

* How should the country manage these dollars?
* How can we get people to spend dollars?
* How do we make placing monies in India not so attractive?

Consequently, we are seeing a host of changes. Indians and Indian companies can purchase companies abroad, have bank accounts and take as much as they want (within reason) when they go abroad. Non-Residents can repatriate up to $1 million per annum for a variety of needs. In short, the rupee is practically convertible. The RBI is also not as encouraging of Non-resident deposits. The rates of interest on Foreign Currency Non Resident Deposits and Non- resident External (NRE) Accounts have been reduced.

India is being seen as a vibrant economy. Its GDP growth as mentioned earlier was over 9% in 2006, and individuals are keen to invest in India in the long term. At the annual summit in Davos, India was on everyone's lips. Indian's are leading large companies too – Nooyi, Mittal et al. Indian companies no longer have difficulty raising money abroad. Indeed, even second rung companies have had public offers abroad which have been well subscribed.

The run continues. GDP growth is likely to be around 9%. Industrial growth is strong. There is considerable international interest in India. The stock market is booming. Even though immediately after the budget the market fell, many believe the Sensex (Bombay Stock Exchange Sensitivity Index) will rise over 20,000 points before Diwali 2007.

Non-Resident Indians continue to be an important and integral part of our society. It is for them that this book is being updated – to make them aware of what the rules and the laws, are and the changes that have come into being. As there have been several changes within the year, I have attempted to give references to various circulars so that there is a point of reference.

Read on ....

Raghu Palat
Mumbai

PREFACE
TO THE FIRST EDITION

March 2007

I have been a Non-Resident several times - in the UK, the US, Asia and Africa. While a Non-Resident, I met others like myself, and one of the factors that bound us and kept us in animated conversation for hours and days together were the laws in India relating to Non-Residents. Many things were unclear such as:

— Who is a Non-Resident?

— What is taxable and what is not?

— Can a Non-Resident buy shares?

— Can a Non-Resident buy property?

— What kinds of bank accounts can a Non-Resident open?

— What can the Non-Resident bring in and take out?

And a host of other similar questions.

As these had puzzled me for years, I did the most logical thing possible. I read all that I could on Non-Resident Indians (NRIs). This book is the result.

One of the issues that I noticed when I began reading on matters pertaining to NRIs was the fact that most books were written in archaic professional language - legalese, taxalese and accountingese. It was difficult for an individual to understand the message being conveyed. This book attempts to surmount that. It is written for the layman, in layman terms and in easily understandable English. The aim of the book is to educate and to enlighten and not to confuse and send one to a consultant or an adviser. Its aim is to make the reader clear on issues pertaining to NRIs.

This book is for the NRI – the individual who goes abroad

to earn and who has an intention of returning to India. It is for the NRI who maintains bank accounts in India. It is for the NRI who visits India periodically. It is for the NRI who owns assets in India.

This book is also for the aspiring NRI – the professional who is planning to emigrate or to work abroad for a few years.

This book is also for the businessman and the tourist who travels abroad. What can he bring in, what can he take out, what should he do?

It is also hoped that this book will be of use to bankers who need to refer to the kinds of accounts that NRIs are permitted to keep and the manner in which they may make investments and how they may repatriate their funds.

This book is also aimed at serving as a reference for students in both business and professional schools.

In short, the purpose of this book is to give you guidance on the rules and laws pertaining to NRIs so that you are better prepared to handle your affairs in India.

This book is, for ease of reading and reference, divided into several parts:

- Initially, the book will define an NRI and the different ways it is defined by the various laws of India.
- Then the reader is introduced to taxation in India - the different kinds of taxes and the rules pertaining to these different types.
- The reader is then advised about the different types of bank accounts that can be kept and the rules pertaining to these.
- Investments that an NRI can make and the rules pertaining to loans and overdrafts are also discussed.
- The reader is then explained the baggage rules and the rules pertaining to the import and export of items.

In short, it contains all the things that, in my experience, an NRI would like to know.

My hope is that by reading this book, you will be clear on the laws and rules as they pertain to NRIs and that when you either visit or go out of India for work or otherwise, you - the reader - are clear about what you can and cannot do, and what you should know. If you are, then the purpose of this book has been realized.

Raghu Palat
Mumbai

INTRODUCTION

During the days before independence those who were in the Indian Civil Service were known as "the twice born". They were the elite, the privileged. They were a class apart from the rest.

The Non-Resident Indian has usurped that position and title. He is definitely the privileged, and to woo him and to honor him, there are distinct rules and benefits for him. He is not "primus inter-pares". He is more equal than other Indians.

The Non-Resident Indian has earned that right, the right to be admired, the right to be looked up to, the right to be honored. He has made a name for himself and done our country proud. Had it not been for him, India would not be as honored as it is today in so many diverse fields - medicine, economics, information technology, engineering, business and a host of other disciplines. Many left India with literally nothing more than the shirts on their backs, they worked in hostile environments, often in pitiable conditions and in difficult situations. In spite of these handicaps, they have not only survived, they have triumphed. Today, they constitute the wealthiest ethnic community in the United States of America, Africa, the Middle East, and in several European countries. The software revolution has made several of them among the richest men in the world. Non-Resident Indians today lead many organizations and in many disciplines – banking, information technology, steel, hospitality and the law. And yet, they have kept to their values, their upbringing, their traditions and their roots. Wealth has not corrupted them. There is much to be admired from the Non-Resident Indian.

Over the years, and especially as NRIs began to be recognized as a significant economic power, many rules and regulations pertaining to them have been passed. In recent times, several of these have been relaxed or repealed. In the ensuing chapters, this book will define an NRI and then discuss issues that pertain to him – taxation, investments, loans, baggage rules and other matters that he needs to know.

NON-RESIDENT 1

WHO IS A NON-RESIDENT? HOW DOES A PERSON BECOME ONE?

The term 'Non-Resident' refers to a person who is not resident in India. Following the repeal of the Foreign Exchange Regulation Act 1973 (FERA), there are two clear but separate definitions – one under the Foreign Exchange Management Act 1999 (FEMA), and the other under the Income Tax Act 1961.

1. UNDER THE FOREIGN EXCHANGE MANAGEMENT ACT (FEMA)

The Foreign Exchange Management Act 1999 (FEMA), replaced the Foreign Exchange Regulation Act (FERA) with effect from June 1, 2000. Sections 2(v) and 2(w) of this Act have the following definitions.

PERSON RESIDENT IN INDIA

(i) A person residing in India for more than 182 days during the course of the preceding financial year but does not include:

(A) A person who has gone out of India or stays outside India, in either case –

— (a) For or on taking up employment outside India, or

— (b) For carrying on a business or vocation outside India, or

— (c) For any other purpose in such circumstances as would indicate his intention to stay outside India for an uncertain period.

(B) A person who has come to India or stays in India, in either case other than–

— (a) for or on taking up employment in India, or

— (b) for carrying on a business or vocation in India, or

— (c) for any other purpose in such circumstances as would indicate his intention to stay in India for an uncertain period:

(ii) Any person or corporate body registered or incorporated in India.

(iii) An office, branch or agency in India owned or controlled by a person resident outside India.

(iv) An office, branch or agency in India outside India owned or controlled by a person resident in India.

PERSON RESIDENT OUTSIDE INDIA

A person who is not resident in India: i.e. a person who stays outside India or has otherwise gone out of India.

(a) for or on taking up employment outside India, or

(b) for carrying on a business or vocation outside India, or

(c) for any other purpose, in such circumstances as would indicate his intention to stay outside India for an uncertain period.

An Indian student who goes abroad to study will be a Non-Resident.

2. UNDER THE INCOME TAX ACT

Tax liability in India is determined by the residential statusof an individual. There are three categories:

(I) Non-Resident

(ii) Not Ordinarily Resident

(iii) Resident

NON-RESIDENT

Under Section 115C (e) of the Income Tax Act 1961, a

Non-Resident Indian means an individual, who being a citizen of India, is not a "resident". Thus, every Indian citizen who is a Non-Resident in India in any previous year is a an NRI.

A person is considered Non-Resident under the Income Tax Act if his stay in India does not exceed the limits specified below in a financial year. In this context, a financial year is considered to be from April 1 to March 31.

If the stay does not exceed

(i)	General rule	59 days
(ii)	Person whose total stay in India during the preceding 4 years has not exceeded 364 days	181 days
(iii)	Year of leaving India for employment outside India (Indian citizens only)	181 days
(iv)	Year of leaving India as a member of the crew of an Indian ship (Indian citizens only)	181 days
(v)	Visits to India (for Indian citizens and persons of Indian origin only)	181 days

An individual of India origin, though not a citizen of India, is also considered as a Non-Resident Indian.

A person is considered to be a person of Indian origin if he or either of his parents or any of his grandparents were born in undivided India. This does not include those in Pakistan or Bangladesh.

NOT ORDINARILY RESIDENT

A resident individual is treated as Not Ordinarily Resident (NOR) if he satisfies either of the following tests:

(i) He has not been a resident in India for nine of the ten preceding years, or

(ii) If he has not been in India for a period of 730 days or more during the preceding seven years.

It was widely held that if a person qualifies as a Non-Resident (under the Income Tax Act) for two successive years, he will be eligible to be considered as an NOR for nine subsequent years.

The advantage of being an NOR is that any foreign income earned in the next subsequent years will be exempted from income tax even if the person is in India for all or most of the time or has returned to India. The foreign income should not have been derived from a business controlled in India or a profession set up in India. This provision came under scrutiny in the Gujarat High Court in the case of Pradip J. Mehta vs. CIT (2002) 256 ITR 647. The Court held that a person can be treated as resident but not ordinarily resident only if he is a Non-Resident for nine out of the ten preceding years.

The Finance Act2003 finally put the issue to rest. It amended Section 6 of the Income Tax Act 1961, stating that with effect from April 1, 2004, "A person is said to be 'Not Ordinarily Resident' in India in any previous year if such a person is –

a) An individual who has been a Non-Resident in India in nine out of the ten previous years preceding that year, or has during the seven previous years preceding that year been in India for a period of, or periods amounting in all to 729 days or less; or

b)A Hindu undivided family whose manager has been a Non-Resident in India in nine out of ten previous years preceding that year, or has during the seven years preceding that year been in India for a period of, or periods amounting in all to 729 days or less."

In short, an individual will now be considered to be an NOR in India in any previous year if he has been Non-Resident in India in nine out of the ten preceding years, or has during the seven preceding years, been in India for a period of 729 days or less.

This implies that as a consequence of the change introduced in Finance Act 2003, the global income of foreign nationals including expatriates, working for multinational companies for two years or more, will become taxable in India. However, expatriates can claim credit in their country of origin for taxes paid in India (if there is a double taxation agreement).

Also, those who are already enjoying NOR status will be deprived of this status from the next financial year, as per the provisions of the Finance Act 2003.

Under the Income Tax Act, the year is from April 1 to March 31.

The day of arrival and the day of departure are considered as days in India. For this purpose, the date stamped on the passport is considered proof. If your flight is at 1.00 a.m. in the morning, it is wise to check in and go through immigration before midnight. It should be noted that the number of days in India are calculated strictly and even one day's excess stay will change a person's status.

RESIDENT IN INDIA

It is also important to be aware of what a resident is. Section 6 (I) of the Income Tax Act 1961, defines a resident as a person who has:

(a) in that year been in India for a period or periods amounting in all to 182 days or more, or

(b) within the four years preceding that year been in India for a period or periods amounting in all to 365 days or more and has been in India for 60 days or more in that year.

The period of 60 days is changed to 182 days in the case of an Indian citizen who leaves India as a member of a crew of an Indian ship or for the purpose of employment outside India. In the case of an Indian citizen who comes to India for business or pleasure or any purpose, 60 days is changed to 182 days. The Central Board of Direct Taxes (CBDT) circular No. 586 dated November 28, 1990, states that the Indian crew members of an Indian ship going to a foreign country would be Non-Residents if they board such ships outside the territorial waters of India for 182 or more days during any year. Seamen will be charged taxes only for the period they are working within Indian waters on coastal ships.

A Hindu Undivided Family (HUF) firm or an association of persons or a body of individuals is resident in India in any previous year except when during that year, the control and management of its affairs are situated wholly outside India. Even if a part of the control and management of the affairs of an HUF or partnership firm or of an association of persons is situated in India, it would be considered to be resident in India (Section 6(2) of the Income Tax Act 1961). An HUF will be treated as 'Not Ordinarily Resident' if the manager of the HUF has not been resident in India in nine out of ten previous years preceding that year and has not during the seven previous years, preceding that year been in India for a period or periods amounting in all to 730 (i.e. two years) or more (Section 6 (6)(b)).

A company is said to be a resident in India in any previous year according to Section 6(3) of the Income Tax Act if it satisfies any of the following two conditions :

(i) It is an Indian company, or

(ii) During that year, the control and management of its affairs is situated wholly in India.

However, any other person is stated to be a resident in India under Section 6(4) of the Income Tax Act in any previous year in every instance except where, during that year, the control and management of its affairs are situated wholly outside

India. There is no distinction as far as non-individual assessees are concerned between a resident and an ordinary resident. If an HUF or a company is registered in India during any previous year, it would also be considered as resident and ordinarily resident in India in that year.

EXAMPLES

1 Let us assume that a person who lived abroad returned to India on May 1, 2006, and again left India on November 10, 2006. Since his stay in India exceeds 181 days, he will be regarded as a resident for the assessment year 2007-2008. However, if his stay in India during the previous four years was less than 365 days and his stay during the previous year 2006-2007 was les than 182 days, he will be regarded as a Non- Resident for the financial year ending on March 31, 2007.

2 Let us assume that Raman Menon came on a visit to India on May 1, 2006, and left on November 10, 2006 (after a stay of more than 181 days). Prior to April 1, 2006, he was in India for more than 365 days during the previous four years. He will be regarded as a resident for the assessment year 2006-2007 as his stay in India during the previous year 2006-2007 was more than 181 days.

3 Let us assume that Raman Menon returned to India on May 1, 2006, on a visit and left after a stay of 165 days. Prior to April 1, 2006, he was in India for over 365 days during the previous four years. In this example, Raman Menon will be regarded as a Non-Resident for the assessment year 2007-2008 as his stay during the previous year was less than 182 days.

4 Let us assume that Raman Menon is a crew-member of an Indian Ship. He leaves India on September 20, 2006, for employment. He comes to India on a visit after April 1, 2007. He was in India for over 365 days during the preceding four years. He will be considered as a Non-Resident despite the fact that he was in India for a period of more than 365 days during the preceding four years and was in India for more than 60 days during the previous year 2006-2007.

5 On the other hand, let us assume that Raman Menon left India on May 1, 1999 and came back to India on August 1, 2003. During the period he was abroad, he visited India every year but his stay did not exceed 181 days. During the period April, 1, 2003, and July 31, 2003, he did not visit India. From August 1, 2003, he settled in India. His status for the various assessment years will be as follows:

Financial Year	Assessment Year	Status
1999-2000 to 2002-2003	2000-00 to 2003-04	Non-Resident
2003-04	2004-05	Resident but Not Ordinarily Resident
2003-05 to 2011-2012	2005-06 to 2012-13	Resident & Ordinarily Resident.

6 Altaf Khan was born in Karachi in undivided India. He left Karachi and went to London in 1946 to study. He married a lady there and settled down. In 1950, a son, Farid, was born to him. Farid Khan visits India on July 22, 2003. As his father, Altaf Khan, was born in undivided India, Farid Khan would be an NRI.

7 Ted Smith is an Englishman. He visits India in June 2007 and stays on to February 2004. As his stay in India is more than 182 days, he would be considered as

a resident for the year 2007-2008.

8 Murali Iyer went to the US to study in May 2006. He returned to India for his brothers wedding on April 3, 2007, and left India on September 11, 2007. He has been in India for four years preceding the financial year 2006-2007 for 365 days or more. Also, he has come on a visit from abroad during the financial year 2007-2008 and has stayed in India for 162 days. He would be considered as a Non-Resident in India for the financial year 2007-2008, relevant to the assessment year 2008-2009.

9 Guru Kamath, a software engineer, leaves India on July 22, 2007, for the first time to the US on business and will be there for two years. As his stay in India in the financial year 20072008 is less than 182 days, the first condition of being a resident in India is not met. He has, however, stayed in India during the preceding four financial years for a period exceeding 365 days or more and has also stayed in India for a period totaling more than 60 days. He would be fulfilling the second condition. However, had he gone on business and not for employment, the period of 60 days would be extended to 182 days. And as he fulfills the second condition, he will be considered as a resident. If he had left India for the purpose of employment, then he would be considered as a Non-Resident in India, as he would have been in India for less than 182 days.

10 Chetan Patani went to Kenya to work in a bank in 1985 and has not been in India for four years. His total stay in India during the preceding seven years was 830 days. He returned to India on January 10, 2007. He was not resident in India for nine of the ten previous years. Thus, even though his stay in India in the preceding

seven years was 830 days, he would not be a Resident and Ordinarily Resident in India. Mr. Patani will be considered as a Resident but Not Ordinarily Resident in India for the assessment year 2008-2009.

However, as per the provisions of the Finance Act, 2003, since his stay during the previous seven years exceeds 729 days, he will be deemed to be a Resident and Ordinarily Resident for the assessment year 2010-11 and onwards.

11 Junaid Merchant went abroad to study in 1985. He visits India regularly. During the ten financial years preceding 2007-2008, he was a Non-Resident in India for nine years. However, his total stay in India during the seven years preceding 2007-2008 was 732 days. He will be a resident in 2007-2008. As he has fulfilled the condition set out in Finance Act 2003, regarding stay exceeding 729 days during the preceding seven years, he would thus be classified as a person who is Resident and Ordinarily Resident in India for the assessment year 2008-2009.

12 Akhil Daruwalla leaves India for the first time to take up a job in Singapore in May 2007. He may not be back for four years. Although Daruwalla has been a resident in India for nine years during the last 10 years preceding 2007-2008, and has also been in India for 730 days or more during the last seven years, he would still not be Ordinarily Resident in India, as he has gone for employment in 2008-2009.

There are tremendous advantages of being classified as an NRI and one must therefore plan one's arrival and departure into/from India to gain the maximum benefit.

Leaving India for the first time

A person is a resident in India in any previous year if he fulfils both the conditions laid down in Section 6(1) of the

Income Tax Act. When leaving India, he can avoid being a resident by timing his departure. An individual who leaves India for the purpose of employment outside India is not considered to be resident in India if his total stay in India during the relevant previous year is only 181 days or less in that year. It is important that a person leaving India for employment leaves India on a date that ensures that his stay in India is less than 182 days. This is available only for people who go for employment outside India and not otherwise. If a person leaves India for business or professional purposes, he will be a resident in India if his stay is 60 days or more during the relevant financial year (if he has been in India for a period amounting to 365 days or more during the four years preceding the relevant financial year).

> These procedures must be taken into account when a person leaves India for the first time and also on subsequent employments.

Examples

- Vishwanath Nair leaves India for the first time to take up a job in Nairobi on September 30, 2007. His stay in India is for 183 days. As this exceeds 181 days, he would be resident in India. If he had left on September 25, 2007, then his residential status would have been different. His stay in India would have been 178 days and he would be a Non-Resident in India for the financial year 2007-2008 relevant to the assessment year 2008-2009.

- Let us take the case of Rajan Pillai who leaves India to start a business in Bangkok, Thailand, on July 8, 2007. He has, prior to this, always been in India. The condition, in this case, of physical residence is 60 days and not 182 days (not leaving to take up employment but to start a business). Rajan has been in India for more than 365 days in the preceding four financial years. He would therefore be a resident for the assessment year 2008 2009. If he had gone to take up employment, he would not have been so.

Visits to India

- When visiting India, a Non-Resident must ensure that he does not stay in India for more than 181 days in a year. In calculating the period of stay, both the day of arrival and the day of departure will be considered. This is applicable only for those whose physical stay in India has been for a period of 365 days or more during the last four previous years preceding the relevant previous year. If the stay of the person has been for 364 days or less during the last four financial years preceding the relevant financial year, he must stay in India for 182 days or more to be a resident.

Return to India

- When returning to India, one must try as much as possible to return fulfilling the conditions of not being Ordinarily Resident in India as laid down in Section 6 (6) of the Income Tax Act 1961. This would ensure that he would not be liable for tax on his foreign income.

Examples

- Amitava Adige has been living in Mombasa, Kenya, for 23 years. He decides, on retirement, to return to India for permanent settlement. He returns on May 3, 2007. He has, for the last ten years, been a Non-Resident. He has a house in London on which he earns rent. The rental income he earns will not be liable for tax in India for the financial year 2007-08, as he has been outside India for at least nine of the last ten years.
- On the other hand, let us assume that Sushil Hegde returned to India after 33 years in May 2007. He had, however, been resident in India for three years, i.e. the financial years 1999-2000, 2000-2001 and 2001-2002. On his return to India,

he will be a Resident and Not Ordinarily Resident for the financial years 2007-08. For the financial years 2007-08 and beyond, he will be a Resident and Ordinarily Resident.

As would be appreciated on account of tax implications, it is imperative that one plans one's visits, stays, departures and arrivals.

PERSONS OF INDIAN ORIGIN 2

There had been a tremendous amount of pressure from Indians of foreign nationality (i.e. foreign nationals of Indian origin) for India to permit dual nationality. This was to enable them to come into India without the need of a visa and to invest.

In his budget speech in 1999, the then Finance Minister stated, "The Government has decided to draw up a scheme for the issuance of a Persons of Indian Origin (PIOs) card for those living abroad and having foreign passports."

Later in 1999, the government launched a scheme for PIOs called the PIO Card scheme. This scheme allows visa-free entry to people of Indian origin and gives them the rights enjoyed by NRIs including the right to purchase non-agricultural land.

In this connection, persons of Indian origin are defined as those whose parents, grandparents or great grandparents (fourth generation) were citizens of undivided India and are now citizens of another country. Those who are Pakistanis or Bangladeshis will not be eligible.

Under the Scheme, PIO cards would be issued to eligible applicants through the concerned Indian embassies/high commissions and consulates and for those staying on a long-term basis (on a long-term visa).

The fee for the card which has a validity of 15 years (subject to the validity of passport) is US$310 for adults and US$155 for children. This was effective from September 15, 2002. Its validity is 15 years from the date of issue. Besides making their journey easier, simpler and smoother, the scheme entitles PIOs a wide range of economic, financial, educational and cultural benefits. The benefits are:

(i) No requirement of a visa to visit India.

(ii) No requirement to register with the Foreigners Registration Officer if continuous stay does not exceed 180 days. If continuous stay does exceed 180 days, then registration is required within 30 days of expiry of 180 days with the Foreigners Registration Officer of the area (or at the district headquarters).

(iii) A PIO card holder enjoys parity with NRIs with respect to all facilities available to the latter in the economic, financial and educational fields. These include:

(a) Acquisition, holding, etc. of immovable property

(b) Admission of children under the NRI quota in educational institutions. These institutions will include Indian Institutes of Technology (IITs) and Indian Institutes of Management (IIMs)

(c) Various housing schemes of the Life Insurance Corporation of India (LIC), State Governments and other Government Agencies

(d) All future benefits to NRIs will also be applicable to PIOs.

PIOs will have no parity in the sphere of political rights. It will not give them voting rights.

The right to buy property will not be valid in Jammu and Kashmir.

PIO cards can also be issued by an officer in an Indian Mission notified for the purpose or the Joint Secretary, Ministry of Home Affairs, or the Foreigners Regional Registration Officer, New Delhi, Mumbai, Kolkata, or the Chief Immigration Officer, Chennai.

PIO cards can be cancelled if:

(1) The PIO card was obtained by fraud, false representation or the concealment of any material fact, or

(2) The PIO card holder has shown himself by act or speech to be disaffected towards the Constitution of India, or

(3) The PIO is a citizen of a country in war with India or committing external aggression against India, or any other country assisting the country at war with or committing such aggression against India, or

(4) The PIO card holder has been sentenced in India for indulging in acts of terrorism, smuggling of narcotics, arms, ammunition, etc., or sentenced for committing an act punishable with imprisonment up to one year.

(5) It is not conducive to the public interest that the individual should have a PIO card.

The addresses of the Registration Offices are:

Delhi: Foreigners Regional Registration Office,
Level II,
East Block VIII,
R. K. Puram,
Sector 1,
New Delhi - 110 002.

Mumbai: Foreign Registration Officer,
Annexe II,
Commissioner of Police,
Crawford Market,
Mumbai - 400 001.

Kolkata: Foreigners Regional Registration Officer,
237, Acharya Jagdish Chandra Bose Road,
Kolkata - 700 020.

Chennai: Chief Immigration Officer,
Bureau of Immigration,
Shastri Bhavan Annexe,
No. 26, Haddows Road,
Chennai - 600 006.

MINISTRY OF HOME AFFAIRS NOTIFICATION

(i) This scheme may be called PIO Card Scheme, 2002;

(ii) It shall come into force with effect from September 15, 2002.

1. Definition: In this scheme, unless the context otherwise requires

   (a) "Indian Mission" means the Embassy of India/High Commission of India/Indian Consulate in a foreign country.

   (b) "Person of Indian origin" means a foreign citizen not being a citizen of Pakistan, Bangladesh and other countries as may be specified by the Central Government from time to time if ;

   (i) He/she at any time held an Indian passport, or

   (ii) He/she or either of his/her parents or grandparents or great grandparents was born in and permanently resident in India as defined in the Government of India Act 1935 and other territories that became part of India thereafter, provided neither was at any time a citizen of any of the aforesaid countries (as referred to in 2(b) above), or

   (iii) He/she is a spouse of a citizen of India or a person of Indian origin covered under (i) or (ii) above.

   (c) "PIO Card" means a card issued under this scheme.

2. Form of application for issue/renewal of a PIO Card:

   An application for issue/renewal of a PIO Card shall be made in the prescribed form and shall be accompanied by documentary evidence to show that the applicant is a person of Indian origin as defined.

3. Authority to which the application is to be made:

   (i) An application for issue of a PIO Card shall be made to an Indian Mission in the country where the applicant is ordinarily resident.

   (ii) Applicants already in India on a long-term visa (more than one year) shall make the application for issue of a PIO Card to the following authorities.

(A) Those residing in:

(a) Delhi

Foreigners Regional Registration Officer, Level II, East Block VIII, R.K. Puram, Sector I, New Delhi 110 002.

(b) Mumbai

Foreigners Regional Registration Officer, Annexe II, Commissioner of Police, Crawford Market, Mumbai 400 001.

(c) Kolkata

Foreigners Regional Registration Officer, 237, Acharya Jagdish Chandra Bose Road, Kolkata 700-020.

(d) Chennai

Chief Immigration Officer, Bureau of Immigration, Shastri Bhavan Annex, No.26, Haddows Road, Chennai 600-006.

(B) Those residing in areas other than (A) above:-

Joint Secretary (Foreigners), Ministry of Home Affairs, 1st Floor, Lok Nayak Bhavan, Khan Market, New Delhi 110-003.

4. Authority to grant a PIO Card:

The authority to grant a PIO Card shall be an officer in an Indian Mission notified for the purpose or the Joint Secretary, Ministry of Home Affairs, Government of India, or the Foreigners Regional Registration Officer (New Delhi, Mumbai, Kolkata), or the Chief Immigration Officer, (Chennai).

5. Validity of PIO Card:

A PIO Card shall be valid for a period of 15 years.

6. Fee:

Fee for a new PIO Card for adults – US$310

Fee for a new PIO Card for children below the age of 18 years – US$155.

Status of PIO Cards issued earlier as per PIO Card Scheme (1999)

PIO Card issued earlier for US$1000 will continue to remain valid and no refund shall be admissible. However, the validity of such cards shall be extended by 10 more years without charging any fee.

7. Facilities to be extended to a PIO Card holder:

(i) A PIO Card holder shall not require a visa to visit India.

(ii) A PIO Card holder will be exempted from the requirement of registration if his/her stay in India does not exceed 180 days.

(iii) In the event of continuous stay in India by the PIO Card holder exceeding 180 days, he/she shall have to get himself/herself registered within 30 days of the expiry of 180 days with the concerned Foreigners Registration Officer at the district headquarter.

(iv) A PIO Card holder shall enjoy parity with NRIs in respect of all facilities available to the latter in the economic, financial and educational fields, except in matters relating to the acquisition of agricultural/plantation properties. No parity shall be allowed in the sphere of political rights.

8. Cancellation of PIO Card:

The Central Government may, by order, cancel the PIO Card, if it is satisfied that:

(a) The PIO Card was obtained by means of fraud, false representation or the concealment of any material fact, or

(b) The PIO Card holder has shown himself by act or speech to be disaffected towards the Constitution of India and other laws of India, or

(c) The PIO Card holder is a citizen or subject of any country at war with, or committing external aggression against India, or of any other country assisting the country at war with or committing such aggression against India; or

(d) The PIO Card holder has been sentenced in India for indulging in acts of terrorism, smuggling of narcotics, arms, ammunitions, etc., or has been sentenced for committing an offence punishable with imprisonment up to one year or fine up to Rs. 10,000, or

(e) It is not conducive to the public interest that the person should continue to hold a PIO Card.

No reasons shall be assigned for withdrawal of the Card.

Status of PIO Cards issued earlier as per PIO Card Scheme (1999)

PIO Card issued earlier for US$1000 will continue to remain valid and no refund shall be admissible. However, the validity of such cards shall be extended by 10 more years without charging any fee.

7. Facilities to be extended to a PIO Card holder:

(i) A PIO Card holder shall not require a visa to visit India.

(ii) A PIO Card holder will be exempted from the requirement of registration if his/her stay in India does not exceed 180 days.

(iii) In the event of continuous stay in India by the PIO Card holder exceeding 180 days, he/she shall have to get himself/herself registered within 30 days of the expiry of 180 days with the concerned Foreigners Registration Officer at the district headquarter.

(iv) A PIO Card holder shall enjoy parity with NRIs in respect of all facilities available to the latter in the economic, financial and educational fields, except in matters relating to the acquisition of agricultural/plantation properties. No parity shall be allowed in the sphere of political rights.

8. Cancellation of PIO Card:

The Central Government may, by order, cancel the PIO Card, if it is satisfied that:

(a) The PIO Card was obtained by means of fraud, false representation or the concealment of any material fact, or

(b) The PIO Card holder has shown himself by act or speech to be disaffected towards the Constitution of India and other laws of India, or

(c) The PIO Card holder is a citizen or subject of any country at war with, or committing external aggression against India, or of any other country assisting the country at war with or committing such aggression against India; or

(d) The PIO Card holder has been sentenced in India for indulging in acts of terrorism, smuggling of narcotics, arms, ammunitions, etc., or has been sentenced for committing an offence punishable with imprisonment up to one year or fine up to Rs. 10,000, or

(e) It is not conducive to the public interest that the person should continue to hold a PIO Card.

No reasons shall be assigned for withdrawal of the Card.

OVERSEAS CITIZEN OF INDIA 3

On January 9, 2003, the then Prime Minister Mr. Atal B. Vajpayee announced, in response to tremendous pressure by Persons Of Indian origin, that citizens of certain countries would be given dual citizenship.

The Citizenship (Amendment) Bill 2003 was introduced by the Government in May 2003 and was passed by Parliament on December 22, 2003.

The Act defines an "overseas citizen of India" as a person who:

- Is of Indian origin, or
- Was a citizen of India immediately before becoming a citizen of a specified country and is registered as an overseas citizen of India by the Central Government.

An overseas citizen:

- Will not be entitled to the rights conferred on a citizen of India
- Will not have the right of equality of opportunity in matters of public appointment
- Will not have voting rights
- Will not be entitled to hold constitutional offices (Member of the Lok Sabha, Rajya Sabha, Legislative Assembly or Council, offices of President, Vice President, Judge of Supreme Court & high Court etc.) and appointment to Public Services (Government Services).

Section 14A of the Act states that the Central Government may compulsorily register every citizen of India and issue the national identity card and the Government may maintain a National Register of Indian citizens and for that purpose establish a National Registration Authority.

The Central Government, on an application made, may register any person as an overseas citizen of India if:

- That person is of Indian origin of full age and capacity and is a citizen of a specified country;
- That a person is of full age and capacity who has obtained the citizenship of a specified country on or after the commencement of the Citizenship (Amendment) Act 2003 and who was a citizen of India immediately before such commencement.
- The person registered as an overseas citizen of India shall be an overseas citizen of India as from the date on which he is so registered.

No person who has been deprived of his Indian citizenship under this Act shall be registered as an overseas citizen of India except by order of the Central Government. For this purpose, the expression "citizen of India" shall mean a citizen of another country who:

- Was eligible to become a citizen of India at the time of commencement of the constitution
- Belonged to a territory that became part of India after the 15th day of August, 1947
- The children and grandchildren of a person covered under clauses (i) and (ii), but does not include a person who is or had been at any time a citizen of Pakistan, Bangladesh or such country as the Central Government may, by notification in the Official Gazette, specify.

Dual citizenship has been extended to people of Indian origin so long as their home countries allow dual citizenship in some form or the other under their local laws. However, citizens of Pakistan and Bangladesh are not eligible to be overseas citizens of India.

No person who has been deprived of his Indian citizenship

will be registered as an overseas citizen of India except by an order of the Government.

The Citizenship (Third Amendment) Rules, 2004 was notified in August 2004. It states among other things that the fee for registration is US$275. Of the fee payable for registration, US$25 will be non-refundable, while the rest will be returned in case the application is rejected.

The overseas citizen will enjoy all the rights of an India citizen except those mentioned earlier. He will not require a visa while visiting India and can buy property and enjoy equality with NRIs in economic, financial and educational fields besides having an overseas Indian passport.

It should be noted that Overseas Citizenship is not a full citizenship of India and, therefore does not amount to dual citizenship or dual nationality.

Certificate of Registration has been awarded from January 2006 onwards.

4

GUIDELINES FOR EMIGRATING INDIANS

Emigrating Indians have to comply with the various formalities while transferring their residence from India with the intention of becoming an NRI. They should be conversant with the position of their assets and liabilities in India.

Bank Accounts

As all bank accounts have to be re-designated as Non-Resident (Ordinary) Accounts, emigrating Indians should inform their bankers and request them to convert the existing accounts to NRO Accounts. No special form has been prescribed for this purpose. A simple letter is enough. Once an account is designated as an NRO Account, the operations in the account are permitted as per the terms and conditions governing NRO Accounts.

1. Amounts may be withdrawn for travel expenses within India. RBI permission is not required.
2. Money in the NRO Account can be used for the payment of the NRI's own travel to and from India as well as for the travel of his wife, children and other dependents on Indian carriers. RBI permission is not required.
3. Professional fees to a consultant can be paid from the NRO Account. No RBI permission is required.
4. If a person going abroad wishes to maintain his parents/relatives in India, the account can be opened jointly with the parents/relatives concerned. He can also have a joint account with residents in India.

It must be borne in mind that that the NRO does not make available foreign exchange to any person resident in India against reimbursement in rupees or in any other manner.

Shares

On becoming an NRI, the individual should write to the company concerned to record the change of status as 'Non-Resident' in their registers. For this purpose, he should furnish the following information to the company:

(a) Nationality

(b) Date of leaving India

(c) Foreign Address

(d) Number of shares held and their face value

(e) Name and branch of the bank where the NRI has a bank account and the account number.

Immovable Property

Indians going abroad whether they remain citizens of India or acquire foreign citizenship are permitted to hold immovable property in India under the provisions of Section 6(5) of FEMA, 1999.

Deposits with Companies

NRIs may continue to keep deposits with the Indian companies including non-banking finance companies (NBFCs) registered with RBI, under the provisions of Section 6(5) of FEMA, 1999.

Mutual Funds

RBI permission is not required to hold units of mutual funds and bonds of the Government.

Gold and Jewelry

RBI permission is not more required to keep gold, jewelry and precious stones in India.

Continuation as a Director

No permission is required by an NRI to continue as a Director of an Indian company. RBI has granted general permission vide Notification No. FEMA 16 / 2000 dated May 3, 2000, to companies in India to make payments in Indian

Rupees to their non-resident (including foreign nationals), non-wholetime directors while on a visit to India on company business such as attending a Board Meeting, towards sitting fees, commission or remuneration by way of monthly or quarterly or annual payments in accordance with the provisions contained in the Company's Memorandum of Association or Articles of Association, or in any agreement entered into by it or in any resolution passed by the company in general meeting or by its Board of Directors. The company shall, however, comply with the requirements of any law, rules, regulations, directions etc. applicable for making such payment. In this connection, it is to be noted that necessary approval from the Central Government under Section 309(4) or Section 310 of the Companies Act, 1956 wherever it applies, should be obtained.

Continuation as a Trustee

The emigrating Indian can continue as a Trustee of a private or public Trust without the permission of RBI.

Continuation as Karta of HUF

The emigrating Indian can also continue as a Karta of an HUF without the permission of RBI.

Compulsory Insurance under Pravasi Bhartiya Bima Yojana

The Government has launched a scheme called Pravasi Bhartiya Bima Yojana, 2003 as a social security and welfare measure for citizens of India going abroad for employment. The scheme applies to all citizens of India who apply for and obtain an emigration clearance. Under the scheme it shall be mandatory for all NRIs with Emigration Check Required (ECR) endorsement on their passports to take an insurance policy from any insurance company operating in India, duly registered with the Insurance Regulatory and Development Authority (IRDA). Such an insurance policy should cover the following:

- Minimum validity period should be two years or the actual period of employment contract, whichever is less.

- Minimum sum assured must be Rs. 2 lakh in the event of death or permanent disability leading to loss of employment while in employment abroad.
- In the case of death, cost of transporting the dead body and economic class return airfare of one attendant should be reimbursed by the insurance company. The reimbursement claim should be filed within 90 days of completion of journey.
- In the event of death or permanent disability within 12 months of taking the policy, due to accident / physical injury, the sum assured will be reimbursed.
- Medical insurance cover of minimum Rs. 50,000 in case of hospitalization of insured worker on grounds of accidental injury/sickness/ailments/diseases provided medical treatment is taken in India. The company should either provide cash-less hospitalization and/or reimburse the actual medical expenses.
- If the insured falls sick or is declared medically unfit for the job and the service contract is terminated within the first six months of the policy actual one-way economy class airfare should be reimbursed.
- If the terms of the employment are substantively changed to the disadvantage of the insured, or if the employment is prematurely terminated within three months, for no fault of emigrant, one-way economy class airfare should be reimbursed.
- Maternity benefit to women emigrants for a minimum of Rs. 20,000 should be given. This may be restricted to actuals, provided treatment is taken in India.
- In the event of death or permanently disability of the insured person, his family consisting of spouse and two dependent children upto 21 years of age shall be entitled to hospitalization cover for a maximum of Rs. 10,000 p.a.

- Policy period may be six months, one year, or two years. The premium should be fair and reasonable. Service tax may be charged extra.

Obtaining Income-tax Clearance

The obtaining of a Tax Clearance Certificate has been relaxed with effect from June 1, 2003.

1. A person not domiciled in India, who has come to India in connection with business, profession or employment and who had income derived from any source in India, is required to obtain a no-objection certificate (NOC) in Form 30B from the prescribed authority before leaving India. Such persons shall furnish an undertaking in Form 30A from his employer or the person through whom he is in receipt of the income, to the effect that the tax payable by such person shall be paid by his employer or the person through whom he receives the income.

   A foreign tourist or a person coming to India for a purpose other than business, profession or employment, is not required to obtain the NOC.

2. A person domiciled in India shall, at the time of his departure from India, furnish the following details in Form 30C to the income-tax authorities or other prescribed authority:

   (a) His permanent account number (PAN)

   (b) The purpose of his visit

   (c) The estimated period of his stay abroad.

   If the individual does not have a PAN, or is not required to obtain a PAN, or does not have taxable income, he shall furnish a certificate in the prescribed form.

3. A person domiciled in India in respect of whom circumstances exist which, in the opinion of the income-tax authority, render it necessary for him to obtain a tax clearance certificate, shall be required to obtain such a certificate before he leaves India. An application for this purpose is to

be made in Form No.31. The certificate is issued in Form No.33 only if there are no outstanding taxes due against him in India or satisfactory arrangements have been made for the payment of such taxes.

Executing a Power of Attorney

An emigrating Indian can give power of attorney to a resident. No permission is required for this purpose. The power of attorney should be executed on stamp paper of appropriate values, applicable to the country of execution. The power of attorney should preferably cover the following aspects:

(i) Portfolio Management

(ii) Bank Accounts

(iii) Application to RBI

(iv) Filing of return and representing before tax authorities

Matters incidental to the above.

An emigrating Indian can give power of attorney to a resident. No permission is required for this purpose. The power of attorney should be executed on stamp paper of appropriate values, applicable to the country of execution. The power of attorney should preferably cover the following aspects:

(i) Portfolio Management

(ii) Bank Accounts

(iii) Application to RBI

(iv) Filing of return and representing before tax authorities

(v) Matters incidental to the above.

5 TAXATION AND THE NON-RESIDENT INDIAN

NRIs must be aware of the various tax laws of India: by planning their tax, they can save a considerable amount of money.

Tax can be saved, as has been discussed, by planning the residential status of the individual. However, income arising in India is liable for tax in India. There are exemptions available, permissible deductions, and tax rebates. The NRI will be wise to be aware of these to reduce the incidence of tax.

What are the direct laws that affect the individual? The more important ones are:

The Income Tax Act 1961: This is the main law that deals with income tax. This is supplemented by the Income Tax Rules 1962.

The Wealth Tax Act 1957: This act determines the wealth tax payable by companies, individuals and Hindu undivided families. This is supplemented by the Wealth Tax Rules, 1962.

Finance Act: The Finance Act amends the tax laws including the rates at which tax is to be levied. This is presented as an Act to Parliament in February/March every year (usually on the last day of February) and then when passed, it becomes an Act.

Circulars: The Central Board of Direct Taxes issues circulars from time to time. These are binding on the authorities, and by extension affect the taxpayer.

Notifications: Notifications are issued by the Government of India and published in the official Gazette. These deal with exemptions or details of a provision or concession.

Income Tax

An NRI is required, under Section 5 (2) of the Income Tax Act, to pay tax on the total income of a particular year derived from whatever source, which:

- Is received or is deemed to be received in India in such a year by or on behalf of such persons, or
- Accrues or arises or is deemed/construed by law to accrue or arise to him in India during such a year.

The following incomes are some instances when the law considers income as having been accrued in India.

(a) Income from business arising through any business connection in India.

(b) Income from property if such property is situated in India.

(c) Income from any asset or source if such asset or source is in India.

(d) Income from salaries if the salary is earned in India. Rendering of service in India amounts to earning the income in India.

(e) Income from salaries payable by the government to a citizen of India even though the services are rendered outside India.

(f) Income by way of interest paid by the government or by any other person in certain circumstances.

(g) Income by way of royalty if payable by the government or by any other person in certain circumstances.

(h) Income by way of fees for technical services if such fees are payable by the government or by any other person in certain circumstances.

Although the following income appears to be arising in India these are construed as not arising in India.

(a) If an NRI running a news agency or publishes newspapers, magazines, etc. earns income from activities confined to the collection of news and views in India for transmission outside India, such income is not considered to have arisen in India.

(b) In the case of a non-resident, no income shall be considered income to have arisen in India if it arises from operations that are confined to the shooting of any cinematography film. This applies to the following types of non-residents:
   (i) An individual who is not a citizen of India
   (ii) A firm which does not have any partner who is a citizen of India, or who is resident in India
   (iii) A company which does not have any shareholder who is resident in India.

The Finance Bill 2007 states the place of rendering service is not relevant for determining taxability in India. The Bill proposes to insert an explanation in Section 9 to clarify that income by way of interest, royalty or fees for technical services deemed to accrue or arise in India will be included in the total income of the non-resident whether or not the non-resident has a residence or a place of business or a business connection in India. This amendment seeks to negate an order of the Supreme Court where it was held that income by way of fees for technical services earned by a non-resident can be chargeable to tax in India only if the services are utilized and rendered in India or are attributable to a permanent establishment of such a non-resident in India.

The Finance Bill 2007 has a new definition of India. Under clause 25A of Section 2 of the Income Tax Act 1961, India is deemed to include the Union Territories of Dadra and Nagar Haveli, Goa, Daman and Diu, and Pondicherry. This clause is proposed to be amended to define India to mean the territory of India as referred to in Article 1 of the constitution, its territorial waters, seabed and subsoil underlying such waters, continental shelf, exclusive economic zone or any other maritime zone as referred to in the territorial waters, continental shelf, exclusive economic zone and other Maritime Zones Act 1976, and the airspace above its territory and territorial waters.

To avoid the difficulties in working out the net income of a non-resident from his gross receipts, the law provides for taxation of most of the income of non-residents on a gross-income basis, which means that the tax liability is determined on the basis of gross receipts without going into the question of expenses incurred in earning those receipts. Such "gross receipt basis" taxation operates in two ways:

(a) By laying down the rate of tax to be applied on gross receipts – The rates are determined at a figure lower than the general rate of tax applicable to total income as it takes account of the possible expenses in earning the income. Such provisions are:

   (i) Tax on dividend (*– other than dividend referred to in Section115O), interest, royalty fee for technical services and income from units (* other than unit holders of open-ended, equity-oriented funds in respect of any distribution made for a period of one year commencing April 1, 2003. Moreover, units of UTI-I are not subject to the dividend distribution tax under Section 115R) (Section 115A).

   (ii) Tax on income and capital gain in respect thereto from units purchased in foreign currency by offshore funds (*– other than unit holders of open-ended, equity-oriented funds in respect of any distribution made for a period of one year commencing April 1, 2003. Also units of UTI-I are not subject to the proposed dividend distribution tax under section 115R) (Section 115AB).

   (iii) Income (*other than dividend referred in Section 115O) and capital gains in respect thereto from bonds and GDRs purchased in foreign currency (Section 115AC).

(iv) Income by way of dividends (*other than dividend referred in Section 115O) from GDRs issued in accordance with employee stock options, notified scheme and income by way of long-term capital gains arising from the transfer of such GDRs in respect of a resident employee of an Indian company or its subsidiary company engaged in specified knowledge based industry or service (Section 115ACA).

(v) Tax on income (*other than dividend referred in Section 115O) of foreign institutional investors from securities (other than those referred in Section 115AB) and capital gains arising from their transfer (Section 115AD).

(vi) Foreign national non-resident sportsmen with regard to income from participation in any game, sport, advertisement or contribution of articles relating to any game or sport in India.

A non-resident sports association with regard to income by way of amount guaranteed to be paid or payable in relation to any game or sport played in India.

(b) By laying down a percentage to be applied on gross receipts to determine the net income. The tax is then calculated at the normal rate of tax on such income. Such provisions are:

(i) Profits of a shipping business (Section 44B).

(ii) Profits of a business of providing services to be used in the business of prospecting, exploration or production of mineral oils (Section 44BB).

The Finance Act 2003, amended the above section and permitted an assessee to claim a lower profit and gain than specified, if he maintained such books of accounts and other documents as required under Section 44AA(2), got his accounts audited, and furnished a report of such audit as required under

Section 44AB; thereon, the assessing officer would proceed to make an assessment of the total income or loss of the assessee under Section 143(3) and determine the sum payable or refundable to the assessee.

(iii) Profits of an operation of aircraft (Section 44BBA).

(iii) Profit from a business of civil construction, etc., in certain turnkey power projects (Section 44BBB).

The Finance Act 2003 omitted the requirement of financing such projects under any international aid program. It has amended the above section and provides that an assessee may claim a lower profit and gain than specified, if he maintains such books of accounts and other documents as required under Section 44AA(2) and gets his accounts audited and furnishes a report of such audit as required under Section 44AB, and thereon, the assessing officer shall proceed to make an assessment of the total income or loss of the assessee under Section 143(3) and determine the sum payable or refundable to the assessee.

In Steffer, Robertson & Kirsten Consulting Engineers and Scientists vs. CIT (230 ITR 206 1998), it was held that amounts paid for preparatory work in a foreign country to a non-resident for services that are to be utilized in India, such amounts would be deemed to accrue or arise in India. It was held that there is no difference between fees for engineering services and amounts paid as living allowances and travel allowances.

In Asian Development Services vs. CIT (239 ITR 713 1999), it was held that in respect of the placement of an amount to a non-resident, tax liability of the non-resident was to be determined with reference to the gross figure.

It must be noted that there is no liability to income tax in India on foreign income merely because it is remitted to India during the year. With regard to non-residents and those resident but not ordinarily resident in India, no income tax is payable by them on income which accrues or arises to them outside India unless it is derived from a business controlled, or any profession set up in India.

Examples

1 Raman Menon is an NRI during the financial year 2007-2008. The income he earns in India (Indian income) is Rs. 55,000. He has earned Rs. 5,00,000 in Kenya. Raman Menon is liable for income tax only on his Indian income of Rs. 55,000. His earnings in Kenya are not liable for tax in India.

2 Narayana Raman earns Rs. 10,00,000 as a salary in Kenya and remits Rs. 6,00,000 to his wife Kumkum who stays in India. As he is an. NRI, there will be no tax payable either on the remittance or the salary he earns.

Let us assume that he is a resident but not ordinarily resident and controls a business in Nairobi from his head office in Mumbai. The income this business earns is Rs. 1,00,000. In addition, he earns Rs. 3,00,000 on investments abroad. Narayana Raman would have to pay tax on the Rs. 1,00,000 that the business earns. However, he will pay no tax on the income on his investments, as he is not ordinarily resident.

Income tax liability is not based on citizenship. Non-citizens are also required to pay tax on income arising in India.

No tax is payable on taxable income of up to Rs. 110,000. Taxable income is arrived at by adding income from all sources and deducting allowable deductions. The amount of tax payable will depend on the various exemptions available and the rates of tax payable at different levels of income.

The tax payable at different levels of income is as follows:

1. On total income up to Rs. 1,10,000 — Nil
2. On total income between Rs. 1,10,001 and Rs. 1,50,000 — 10%

3. On total income between Rs. 1,50,001 and Rs. 2,50,000 — 20%
4. On total income in excess of Rs. 2,50,001 — 30%

On income above Rs. 10,00,000 a surcharge of 10% has to be paid.

In addition education cess at 3% must be paid on income tax and surcharge.

There are three types of tax concessions:

- Incomes totally exempted from tax
- Deductions from taxable income
- Tax rebates.

When certain income is totally exempted from income tax, it is not included in the computation of income tax. These are detailed in Section 10 of the Income Tax Act. There are certain expenses and deductions, which can be deducted from income to arrive at the taxable income. There are also rebates from taxes, i.e. a percentage of certain expenses/investments qualify for claiming a rebate from the tax liability.

It is to be noted that while the slabs (levels of income) mentioned above are applicable to residents and non-residents, non-residents can opt for special procedures in the calculation of income tax in respect of the same sources of income.

Income exempted from Income Tax under Section 10 specific to Non-Residents

- Interest on Non-Resident External Accounts
- Interest on National Savings Certificates (issued before June 1, 2002)
- Certain remuneration of Non-Residents, such as:

  Remuneration received as an employee of a foreign enterprise for services rendered by him during his stay in India, provided that the foreign enterprise is not engaged in any trade or business in India and that his stay does not exceed 90 days.

- Remuneration of Non-Residents even though they are Indian citizens earning from employment outside India.
- Agricultural income: If a person has other income, this will be aggregated for tax purposes to arrive at a rate of tax.
- Certain income such as interest on:
  1. Twelve-year National Savings Annuity Certificates
  2. Treasury Savings Deposit Certificates
  3. Post Office Cash Certificates
  4. National Plan Certificates
  5. National Plan Savings Certificate
  6. Post Office National Savings Certificates
  7. Post Office Savings Bank Accounts (up to a maximum of Rs. 2,250)
  8. Post Office Cumulative Time Deposits
  9. Scheme of Fixed Deposits governed by the Government Savings Certificate (Fixed Deposits) Rules 1968
  10. Scheme of Fixed Deposits governed by the Post Office (Fixed Deposits) Rules 1968
  11. NRI Bonds 1988 issued by the State Bank of India
  12. NRI Bonds (Second Series) issued by the State Bank of India
  13. 10.5% Tax-free Bonds of HUDCO
  14. 9.25% Tax-free Bonds issued by Rural Electrification Corporation Ltd
  15. 10.5% Secured, redeemable, non-convertible, tax-free Bonds issued by National Hydroelectric Power Corporation
  16. Interest payable by a public company registered in India with the main object of providing long-term finance for purchase or construction of residential

houses and eligible for deduction under Section 36(i) (viii). The Finance Act 2003, proposes that this concession be allowed on monies borrowed on or before June 1, 2003

17. Interest on Gold Deposit Bonds issued under the Gold Deposit Scheme, 1999, notified by the Central Government
18. Interest on Bonds issued by a local authority and specified by the Central Government by notification
19. Interest on deposits from Non-Resident (Non-repatriable) Rupee Deposit Schemes (discontinued with effect from April 1, 2002)
20. Resurgent India Bonds
21. India Millennium deposits
22. 10.50% Konkan Railway Bonds
23. Interest on Public Provident Fund Deposits.

- Scholarships granted to meet the cost of education (Section 10(16)).
- Any amount, not exceeding Rs. 5 lakh received or receivable by certain employees on their voluntary retirement or termination of their service need not be included in their total income (Section 10(10C)).
- Sums received from a life insurance policy including bonus other than key-man insurance and a pension plan (Section 10(10D)). Any sum received under an insurance policy in respect of which premium paid during the year exceeds 20% of the actual capital sum assured, shall not be exempted. However, such sum received on death of the person shall be exempted.
- In the case of a minor's income clubbed with that of his parents' under Section 64(1A), the extent to which such income is clubbed or Rs. 1,500 whichever is less (Section 10(32)).

- The Finance Act 2003, inserted Section 10(33) to provide that any income arising from the transfer of a capital asset, being a unit of unit scheme, 1964, referred to the Unit Trust of India (Transfer of Undertaking and Repeal) Act 2002, and where the transfer of asset takes place on or after April 1, 2002, shall be exempted from tax.
- The Finance Act 2003, inserted Section 10(34) to provide that any income by way of dividends referred to in Section 115O, shall not be included in computing the total income of any person.
- Clause (35) of Section 10 provides that any income by way of income received in respect of units from an administrator of the specified undertaking or the specified company or a mutual fund specified under Section 10(23D) shall be exempted.
- The Finance Act 2003 inserted a new clause (36), to provide that any income arising from transfer of a long-term capital asset, being equity shares in a company listed on any recognized stock exchange in India and acquired on or after March 1, 2003 but before March 1, 2004, shall be exempted from tax.
- The Finance Act 2004 abolished long-term capital gains tax and taxed short-term capital gains at a flat 10%.

Income-based deductions

Earlier, there have been various deductions permitted for payments made to pension funds, life insurance premia, and the like. In addition certain income received was not fully taxable. To make this more logical and less complicated, the Finance Act 2005 inserted an income donation aggregating Rs. 1,00,000 abolishing deductions and rebates.

Deductions allowed to Non-Residents

As a general rule, an NRI is not allowed any deductions under Chapter VI-A of the Income Tax Act in computing his total taxable income which is from investment income from foreign exchange assets. An NRI can opt not to be governed by the special provisions relating to taxation of the investment income at the uniform rate of 20% but be governed by the general provisions of the Income Tax Act. Further tax at the uniform rate of 20% on income from house property, etc. to which the general provisions of Chapter XII A of the Income Tax Act does not apply, is not liable. In case of such income, the net income after deducting the expenses for earning such income and certain other deductions is taxable.

Under 80 CCC, contributions to pension plan of the Life Insurance Corporation or any other insurer approved by the Insurance Regulatory and Development Authority (IRDA), up to Rs. 10,000 is deductible for tax purposes.

Deductions up to Rs. 15,000 (Rs. 20,000 for senior citizens is allowed) under Section 80D in respect of medical insurance premiums paid by cheque by an individual. The premiums must be paid on behalf of the assessee, spouse, dependant children, or parents. Mediclaim policy taken by a person going abroad as a protection during his stay abroad does not attract any tax deduction.

Expenditure on treatment of some specified protracted diseases by a resident individual for himself or a dependant relative is permitted as a deduction under Section 80DDB of Rs. 40,000 or the amount actually incurred whichever is less. (Rs. 60,000 for senior citizens).

Under Section 80E, repayment of a loan and interest thereon by an individual taken from a bank or a notified financial institution or any approved charitable institution for higher studies is deductible up to a ceiling of Rs. 40,000 per year for eight successive years. This facility is available on interest paid on a loan taken to educate a relative also.

Under Section 80G, deduction is permitted on the qualifying amount of donations to certain funds in computing total income. In respect of certain donations, the maximum amount eligible is 10% of the gross total income.

Under Section 80-IA, tax holiday is also provided to enterprises providing infrastructure facilities, telecommunication services, industrial parks, power generation, transmission and distribution, and units that develop special economic zones.

- A 10-year tax holiday is available for enterprises engaged in providing infrastructure facility set up on or after April 1, 1995.
- A 5-year tax holiday for undertakings engaged in providing telecommunication services and a deduction of 30% of the profits for the next five years, commencing operations between the period, April 1, 1995 to March 31, 2004.
- Undertakings which develop and operate industrial parks or undertakings engaged in power generation and distribution or development, *maintenance and operation of special economic zones*, are allowed a deduction of 100% of the profits for 10 years (units set up before March 31, 2006). (*The Finance Bill Act 2003, has done away with the requirement of maintenance and operation of SEZs*)

  The Finance Act, 2003 provides that where an undertaking develops a special economic zone on or after April 1, 2001 and transfers the operation and maintenance to another undertaking (transferee undertaking), the deduction to the transferee undertaking shall be available for the remaining period in the 10 consecutive assessment years, as if the operation and maintenance were not so transferred to the transferee undertaking. This amendment is retrospectively applicable with effect from assessment year 2002-03.

Under Section 80-IB, a partial tax holiday is allowed in respect of profits and gains of a new industrial undertaking other than infrastructure development undertaking.

- Profits derived from the operation of a ship brought into use after March 31, 1991 but before April 1, 1995 – 30% of the profits deductible for 10 years.
- A hotel set up between April 1, 1997 to March 31, 2001 or an approved hotel, which starts functioning from that date. In respect of approved hotels, the permissible deduction is 50% of the profits derived; in other cases, a deduction of 30% is allowable.
- Industrial undertakings located in an industrially backward state commencing production between April 4, 1993 and March 31, 2002 are allowed a deduction of 100% for five years and 30% for the next five years (25% for non-company assessees).
- Industrial undertakings located in an industrially backward district of category A and commencing operations between April 1, 1994 and March 31, 2002 are allowed a deduction of 100% for five years and 30% for the next five years (25% for non-company assessees)
- Industrial undertakings located in industrially backward districts of category B and commencing operations between April 1, 1994 and March 31, 2002 are allowed a deduction of 100% for three years and 30% for the next five years (25% for non-company assessees)
- A company engaged in scientific and industrial research and approved after March 31, 2000 but before April 1, 2004 – 100% of the profits for a period of 10 years.
- An undertaking engaged in production (on or after April 1, 1997) and refining (on or after October 1, 1998) of mineral oil is allowed a deduction of 100% of the profits for the first seven years.
- An undertaking engaged in developing and building housing projects approved by a local authority after October 1, 1998 but before March 31, 2005 is allowed a deduction of 100% of the profits. The Finance Act 2003 removed the time limit for completion of the project.

- Undertakings setting up and operating a cold chain facility for agriculture produce (set up between April 1, 1999 to March 31, 2004) are permitted a deduction of 100% for five years and 30% for the next five years. (25% for non-corporate assessees).
- An industrial undertaking which is an SSI (Small Scale Industry) unit engaged in manufacturing or operating a cold storage plant set up between April 1, 1995 and March 31, 2002 is allowed a deduction of 30% for 10 years.
- Undertakings engaged in the integrated handling, storage and transportation of food grains are allowed a deduction of 100% for first five years and 25% for the next five years, which is increased to 30% in case of companies. (Commencing on or after April 1, 2001).
- A multiplex theatre or convention center constructed between April 1, 2002 to March 31, 2005 is allowed a deduction of 50% of the profits for five years.
- Undertakings engaged in refining or production of mineral oil, undertakings engaged in developing and building houses and those engaged in the integrated business of handling, storage and transportation of food grains.
- The Finance Act 2004 permitted a 100% deduction for five years and 25% for the next five years from profits derived by agro-based industries.
- Industrial undertakings set up in Jammu and Kashmir will be eligible for a 100% deduction for five years and 25% for the next five years from profits derived by agro-based industries.

The Finance Act 2003 inserted a provision in Sub-section (4) of Section 80IB, so as to provide that no deduction under the sub-section would be allowed for the assessment year beginning April 1, 2004 or any subsequent year to any undertaking or enterprise referred to in Sub-section (2) of Section 80IC inserted by Clause 35 of the Act.

The Finance Act 2003 also inserted a new section, Section 80IC, in respect of certain undertakings in the states of Sikkim, Uttaranchal, Himachal Pradesh, and the North-Eastern states.

Under Section 80L, a deduction of up to a maximum of Rs. 15,000 in respect of income/interest from government securities, debentures of a cooperative society, deposits under the National Deposit Scheme, deposits with banks and approved financial corporations, deposits with a cooperative society, deposits with housing boards, post office (monthly income) accounts and other specified investments/savings is available. Of this, a deduction of Rs. 3,000 is available for interest on government securities.

The Finance Act 2003, inserted a new section, Section 80QQB, for deduction in respect of income of resident individuals from authorship of books of literary, artistic or scientific nature or royalties or copyright fees (whether receivable in lump sum or otherwise) in respect of such books. This deduction is restricted to a maximum of Rs. 3 lakh. Also where the income from royalty is not in the form of a lump sum consideration in respect to all rights of the assessee in the book, so much of the income before allowing expenses attributable to such income, as is in excess of 15% of the value of the books sold during the previous year shall be ignored. Further, this deduction is also allowable in respect of the income earned from a source outside India that is brought in convertible foreign exchange to India within six months of the end of the financial year or such further time as may be allowed by the competent authority.

Income received in foreign currency by some specified Indian nationals or residents enjoy a deduction of 15% of such income (for the annual year 2004-05) as is brought to India by or on behalf of them in convertible foreign exchange within a period of six months from the end of the year (Sections 80R, 80RR, and 80RRA).

The Finance Act 2003, vide Section 80RRB, permits a

deduction in respect of royalty on patents to resident individuals on patents registered on or after April 1, 2003 subject to a maximum of Rs. 3 lakh. Further, this deduction is also allowable in respect of so much of income earned from a source outside India, as is brought in convertible foreign exchange to India within six months of the end of the financial year or such further time as may be allowed by the competent authority.

All business expenditure can be deducted.

Rebates

The Finance Act 2005 replaced these by the income-based deduction mentioned above.

A rebate is a reduction allowed from the tax liability of an individual. Under Section 88, a rebate is allowed on payment of life insurance premium, contribution to a public provident fund or investment in national savings certificates, etc. up to an amount of Rs. 70,000. The quantum of rebate available to an individual or an HUF is as under:

(i) If the gross total income of an individual is less than Rs. 1.5 lakh, the rebate is at the rate of 20% of the eligible amount.

(ii) If the gross total income exceeds Rs. 1.5 lakh and is less than Rs. 5 lakh, a deduction is at the rate of 15% of the eligible amount.

(iii) If the gross total income exceeds Rs. 5 lakh, then no rebate is allowed.

(iv) A higher deduction of 30% is allowable in case of individuals whose income under the head 'salaries' before allowing deduction under Section 16 does not exceed Rs. 1 lakh and the salary income constitutes 90% of the gross total.

Certain infrastructure investments (including units of any mutual fund dedicated to the infrastructure or telecommunications or power sector or shares/debentures of power and infrastructure companies) qualify for an additional

Rs. 30,000 (Konkan Railway, ICICI Infrastructure Bonds). Thus, an individual can invest up to Rs. 1 lakh in eligible schemes and avail rebate on tax payable.

Any payment made by an individual inclusive of stamp duty, registration fee or other expenses incurred on transfer, towards repayment of sums borrowed from some specified sources for the purpose of construction of a residential house property (not necessarily self occupied) qualifies for a deduction within an overall ceiling of Rs. 20,000 within the overall limit of Rs. 70,000 stated in Section 88.

The Finance Act 2003 allows a rebate on the tuition fees (excluding donation or development fees) paid on full-time education within India of two children of an individual subject to a maximum of Rs. 12,000 per child.

A senior citizen (more than 65 years of age) is also allowed a rebate of up to Rs. 15,000 under Section 88B, i.e. senior citizens are not liable to pay any tax if the total income does not exceed Rs. 1,30,000.

The Finance Act 2003 enhanced the limit of rebate allowed to Rs. 20,000 and thus senior citizens will now not have to pay any tax on an income up to Rs. 1,53,000.

All women below the age of 65 are entitled to a rebate of Rs. 5,000 under Section 88C. This has been abolished by the Finance Bill 2005 and in its place women are to get a higher exemption limit (Rs. 125,000)

Exemption Limits and Tax Incidence of Non-individuals

The exemption limit for an HUF is Rs. 110,000.

A partnership firm is liable for tax at the rate of 30% (until last year - 35%) plus surcharge at the rate of 10% (last year – 2.5%).

A non-resident company is liable to pay income tax on its total income at 40% (plus surcharge of 2.5%). Certain special incomes of a non-resident from royalty and technical fees are, however, liable for tax at a concessional rate of 20% in some cases.

Example

Raman Menon has income from bank deposits of Rs. 30,000, interest on a deposit in a non-resident account of Rs. 5,000 and net income from house property of Rs. 53,000.

Raman Menon's tax liability for the assessment year 2008-09 will be:

	Rs.
Interest from bank deposit	30,000
Interest from a Non-Resident external account exempt under Section 10 (4A)	Nil
Income from house property	53,000
	83,000
Less: Income based deduction	
Bank interest	30,000
Total taxable income	53,000
Income tax	Nil

Tax on a non-resident entity such as HUFs, Partnership Firms, etc.

The exemption limit in the case of an HUF is Rs. 110,000.

Partnership firms are liable to pay tax at 30% and a non-resident company is expected to pay tax on its total income at 40%. Certain special incomes are chargeable at a lower rate of 20%.

Heads of Income

The heads of income chargeable to tax in India are:

1. Salaries
2. Income from house property
3. Profits and gains from business/profession
4. Capital gains
5. Income from other sources.

Computation of Taxable Income

Mohan Panicker, an NRI, worked in India for 90 days in the financial year 2006-2007 and the amount he earned was as follows:

	Rs.
Salary	45,000
Rent received (net)	24,000
Dividend on shares	40,000
Interest on bank deposits	57,000

His taxable income would be:

		Rs.	Rs.
Gross salary			45,000
Rents received		24,000	
Less repairs under Section 24(i)	30%	7,200	16,800
Dividends earned		40,000	
Less: Exempt u/s. 10(34)		40,000	Nil
Gross interest		57,000	
Less permitted under income based deductions		57,000	Nil
TOTAL TAXABLE INCOME			61,800

There will be no tax as the income is below Rs. 1,10,000.

The Clubbing Provisions

Under the Income Tax Act and the Wealth Tax Act, there are provisions whereby the income of the spouse/minor child arising out of gifts given by the assessee would be clubbed with the assessee's income. It is therefore important to be aware of the clubbing provisions of the Act in order to avoid income being clubbed.

Income from Joint Accounts or Joint Investments

Often a husband and wife maintain joint accounts or shares, and investments are purchased in joint names. The issue is whether the income is of one spouse or the other or of both. The mere fact that an account is held jointly or that an investment is held by two or more persons will not affect the liability to tax. The factor that decides the onus of taxation is ownership, i.e. who owns the asset? If an NRI has invested his money jointly with his wife or placed it in a joint account, ownership will remain with the NRI and he will be liable for tax (if any).

When is Income liable to be clubbed?

Under Section 64 (1) (iii), salary, commission, fees or other forms of remuneration whether in cash or in kind, received by the wife of a non-resident from a concern in which the NRI has a substantial stake, then income would be liable to be added to the income of the NRI. This provision will not apply if the wife is technically or professionally qualified and the income is attributable to her technical or professional qualifications. In the case of a company, if equity shares with 20% or more of voting power are owned beneficially by NRIs or by NRIs along with their relatives, the NRI will be deemed to have a substantial stake in the company. In partnerships and associations of persons (AOPs), the NRI would be considered having a substantial stake if he along with relatives is entitled to 20% or more of the profits. Therefore, in any organization where an NRI and his relatives are substantially interested, no remuneration should be paid to the wife unless she is technically/professionally qualified. If this is not so, the income of the spouse will be added to the income of the NRI.

Under Section 64 (1) (iv), income from any gifts made to the spouse will be added to the gifting spouse's income. This will not take place if a transfer of money or funds takes place between the spouses for adequate consideration. Clubbing will occur if a transfer of assets takes place in connection with an agreement to live apart. A gift made by a groom before the wedding will not be clubbed.

Under Section 64 (1) (vii), a gift made by any other person or to trustees for the benefit of the spouse of an NRI would be liable for tax in the hands of the donor spouse. An NRI should therefore not make a gift directly or indirectly for the benefit of the spouse.

Under Section 64 (1A), in computing total income, the entire income accruing to a minor child would be included in the assessee's income. Therefore, the income of a minor child from gifts made by anyone and not necessarily the parents or grandparents only, by way of interest income or rental income on investments made out of the funds of a minor child would be clubbed with the income of the parent. The clubbing provision would not apply if the income of the minor child is from:

- Manual work done by him or
- Activity involving the application of his skill, talent or specialized knowledge and experience.

The clubbing provision would not apply for disabled children suffering from a disability recognized in Section 80 U.

With regard to parents' income, the clubbing would be done with the income of the parent who has a higher income. However, if the parents are divorced, then the clubbing would be with the parent who maintains the child. It should be noted that there is complete exemption of income of Rs. 1,500 per child under Section 10 (32).

It is also to be noted that where the minor is a partner, the share income of a minor who is given the benefits of a partnership will not be clubbed with the parent but is exempted under Section 10 (2A).

Under Section 64 (1) (vi), if a daughter-in-law receives any gift from her parent-in-law, the income arising is the income of the person who has made the gift.

If at any time in a year, a child becomes a major, he is considered a major for the entire period of the year, i.e. the whole year and not for the income after becoming a major.

Under Section 64 (2), when any individual who is part of an HUF converts his self-acquired property into HUF property, the income from this is deemed to arise to the individual and not to the family (HUF).

An NRI does not need to pay income tax on the full income of any property jointly owned by him and his wife provided that his wife's share is not from a gift made by him. NRIs should avoid making gifts to their spouses as the income and wealth could be clubbed.

Remittance of Current Income

Current income earned such as interest, dividends and rent can be remitted outside India.

Difference between Financial Year and Assessment Year

It is important to differentiate between a financial year and an assessment year. Let us take the period April 1, 2006 to March 31, 2007. This will be the financial year 2006-2007. However, for tax purposes it would be the assessment year 2007-2008 as the assessment year takes place only after the completion of the financial year. Thus, in the assessment year 2007-2008, the income for the financial year 2006-2007 is considered. This is also known as the 'previous year'.

6 TAXATION OF INCOME FROM REMUNERATION OF NON-RESIDENTS/ NON-CITIZENS

Normally, remuneration received in India by NRIs is taxable. However, there are some special provisions.

Tax paid on behalf of Non-Residents (Section 10 (6A), (6B), (6C))

Section 10(6A): In the case of a foreign company, tax paid by the government or an Indian entity on payment of royalty or fees for technical services under an approved agreement entered before June 1, 2002.

Section 10(6B): In the case of a non-resident or of a foreign company, tax paid by the government or an Indian concern on any payment other than salary, royalty or technical fees under an approved agreement entered before June 1, 2002.

Section 10(6C): Any income by way of fees for technical services and royalty arising to the foreign company as the government may notify, received in pursuance of an agreement entered into with the central government for providing services in or outside India in projects connected with the security of India.

Remuneration received by Non-Resident Consultants and their Foreign Companies (Section 10 (8A), (8B), (9))

Section (10(8A)): Remuneration of a consultant engaged under a technical assistance program which is paid out of funds made available to an international organization under a technical assistance grant agreement between such organization and the foreign government is exempted from tax. Any other income of such person, which accrues outside India and is not deemed to accrue or arise in India, is also exempted from tax if such income has suffered tax in the country of accrual.

Section 10(8B)): In case of an individual who is assigned to duties in India in connection with any technical assistance program and project in accordance with an agreement entered into by the central government and the international organization referred under Clause 8A.

Section 10(9): Any other income of any family members of any individual referred in Clause (8), (8A), (8B) accompanying such individual, which accrues to them outside India and is not deemed to accrue or arise in India, is also exempted from tax if such income suffers tax in the country where it accrues.

Section 44DA: This relates to special provision for computing income by way of royalties, etc., in the case of non-residents. The section provides that the income by way of royalty for technical services received from the government or an Indian concern in pursuance of an agreement made by a non-resident (not being a company) or a foreign company with the government to the Indian concern after March 31, 2003, where such a non-resident (not being a company) or a foreign company carries on business in India through a permanent establishment situated therein, or performs professional services from a fixed place of profession situated therein, and the right, property or contract in respect of which the royalties or fees for technical services are paid is effectively connected with such permanent establishment established or fixed place of profession, as the case may be, shall be computed under the head 'profits & gains of business or profession' in accordance with the provisions of the Income Tax Act. However, it is provided that no deduction shall be allowed in respect of any expenditure or allowance which is not wholly and exclusively incurred for the business of such permanent establishment or fixed place of profession in India, or in respect of amounts, if any, paid (otherwise than towards reimbursement of actual expenses) by the permanent establishment to its head office or any of its other offices.

The section also requires that all non-residents (not being a company) or a foreign company shall keep and maintain books of accounts and other documents in accordance with the provisions contained in Section 44AA and get the accounts audited by an accountant as defined in the explanation below Sub-section 288 and furnish along with the return of income, a report of such audit duly signed and verified by such accountant.

TAXATION OF BUSINESS INCOME 7

Business income is taxable in the hands of NRIs only when it is either received in India or when it accrues in India.

Income from business operations is construed as accrued in India if it accrues or arises whether directly or indirectly through or from any business connection in India. A business connection, in this context, involves the concept of a control, supervision or an activity of continuous nature. It necessitates a nexus between the activity and the business. A stray transaction or business activity does not, therefore, generally establish such a nexus. Business, on the other hand, means activities carried on continuously and systematically by a person by the application of his labor and skill with a view to earn an income. Unless there is something to establish a relationship between the activity and such continuous and systematic carrying-on of activities, the requisite nexus will be lacking. Instances of an NRI having a business connection in India are:

(a) Maintaining a branch office in India for the purchase or sale of goods or for transacting other business.

(b) Appointing an agent in India for the systematic and regular purchase or raw materials or other commodities or sale of goods or other business purposes.

(c) Erecting a factory in India where the raw material purchased locally is worked into a form suitable for export outside.

(d) Forming a local subsidiary company to sell the products of the non-resident parent company.

(e) Having financial association between a resident and a non-resident company.

An NRI will not be liable for tax in India on any income attributable to operations confined to purchase of goods in India for export even though the NRI has an office or an agency in India for this purpose.

Where an NRI has an agent in India but makes sales directly to Indian customers, there will be no business connection even if he pays his agent an overriding commission on such sales to India provided:

(i) The making of these sales can in no way be attributed to the existence of the agency or to any trading advantage or benefit accruing to the principal from the agency.

(ii) The contracts to sell are made outside India.

(iii) The sales are made on a principal-to-principal basis.

The Finance Act 2003 inserted an explanation in Clause (i) of Section 9(1) so as to remove any doubts regarding 'business connection' and to provide that the expression of 'business connection' shall include any business activity carried out through a person, acting on behalf of the NRI, who -

(i) Has and habitually exercises in India an authority to conclude contracts on behalf of the NRI, unless his activities are limited to the purchase of goods or merchandise on behalf of the NRI; or

(ii) Has no such authority, but habitually maintains in India a stock of goods or merchandise from which he regularly delivers goods or merchandise on behalf of the NRI; or

(iii) Habitually secures orders in India, mainly or wholly for the NRI or for that NRI and other NRIs controlling, controlled by, or subject to the same common control as that NRI.

The expression 'business connection', however, shall not be held to be established in cases where the NRI carries on business through a broker or general commission agent of an independent status, if such a person is acting in the ordinary course of his business.

The Finance Act 2003 also inserted Explanation 3 so as to provide that the broker, general agent or any other agent (referred to as a commission agent) shall be deemed to have an independent status where "such commission agent does not work mainly or wholly for the non-resident and other non-residents controlling, controlled by or subject to the same common control as that non-resident".

Bilateral, double-tax avoidance agreements require the presence of a somewhat permanent nature of the NRI to be able to exercise the jurisdiction of taxing the business income. Such presence is established through the existence of a fixed place of business (permanent relationships). These are:

(a) A place of management
(b) A branch
(c) An office
(d) A factory
(e) A workshop
(f) A mine, oil well or other place of extraction of natural resources
(g) A building site or construction or assembly project which exists for an agreed period
(h) Provision of supervising activities for a minimum agreed period on a building site or construction or assembly project.

Permanent establishment does not include:

(a) The use of the facility solely for the purpose of storage or display of goods or merchandise belonging to the enterprise.
(b) The maintenance of stock of goods or merchandise solely for the purpose of stock or display.
(c) The maintenance of stock of goods or merchandise solely for the purpose of processing by another enterprise.
(d) The maintenance of a fixed place of business solely for the purpose of purchasing goods or merchandise or for

collecting information for the enterprise.

(e) The maintenance of stock of a fixed place of business solely for the purpose of advertising of similar activities, which have a preparatory or auxiliary character for the enterprise.

Only that part of the profits which can be attributed to an activity through 'business connection' or 'permanent establishments' can be the subject matter of tax in India.

The net income from business income is worked on after taking into account normal expenses. An NRI is also entitled to deduct out of gross business income that part of the head office expenses which can be attributed to the Indian operations through business connection or permanent establishment.

The head office expenses deduction is limited to 5% of the adjusted total income (total income before taking account of depreciation, carried forward losses, etc. or deductions).

The income of the following persons is not subjected to tax as it is not considered as accruing or arising in India:

(a) Income of an NRI shall not be deemed to accrue or arise in India from the mere purchase of goods in India for export.

(b) Income of an NRI engaged in the business of running a news agency or of publishing newspapers, magazines or journals arising from activities which are confined to the collection of news and views in India for transmission out of India.

(c) Income of an NRI who is also a citizen of India, or of a firm in which no partner is a resident or an Indian citizen, or of a company in which no shareholder is a resident or an Indian citizen if such income arises from operations which are confined to the shooting of any cinematography film in India.

Profits of Non-Residents from Occasional Shipping Business

Before the departure from any part in India of any ship, the master of the ship has to prepare and furnish to the assessing officer a return of the full amount paid or payable to the owner or charterer or any person on his behalf on account of such carriage since the last arrival of the ship at that port. The assessing officer may allow the ship to depart without furnishing the said return if satisfactory arrangements for filing of returns and payment of taxes are made. In such a case, the return should be filed within 30 days of the departure of the ship. On receipt of the return, the assessing officer will assess the income at 7.5% of the amount stated above and determine the tax at the rate applicable to a foreign company and such sum shall be payable by the master of the ship. Port clearances shall not be granted until the tax has been paid or satisfactory arrangements have been made for the payment thereof. It is open to the NRI to seek a regular tax assessment of such income by furnishing a return of his total income in India before the expiry of the assessment year immediately following the financial year in which the ship departed from an Indian port. In such a case, the tax already paid during the financial year is treated as an advance payment of income tax and is credited to the taxpayer against his final tax liability determined as assessment.

Flat Rate on Gross Receipts

To facilitate assessment and to avoid difficulties involved in adducing evidence to the satisfaction of the assessing officer, taxable business profits of the following persons are computed not on an actual basis but by applying a prescribed rate on gross receipts.

Profit and Gains of Shipping Business (Section 44B)

Profit of NRIs from shipping business is determined by applying a flat rate of 7.5% on:

(i) The amount payable (whether in or out of India) to the assessee or to any person on his behalf on account of the carriage of passengers, livestock, mail or goods shipped at any port of India including amount by way of demurrage or handling charges or amount of similar nature.

(ii) The amount received or considered as received in India by or on behalf of the assessee on account of the carriage of passengers, livestock, mail or goods shipped at any port outside India including amount by way of demurrage or handling charges or any other amount of a similar nature.

Profits and Gains of business of Exploration, etc., of Mineral Oils (Section 44BB)

The income of an NRI assessee from the business of providing services or facilities in connection with, or supplying plant and machinery on hire for use in the business of prospecting for, or extraction or production of mineral oils in India is computed at a sum equal to 10% of the following receipts, in:

(i) Amount paid or payable (in or out of India) on account of services and facilities provided to or on account of supply of plant and machinery on hire to be used in such business

(ii) Amount of the income described above received or receivable in India.

The Finance Act 2003 provided that an assessee may claim lower profits and gains than specified if he keeps and maintains such books of accounts and other documents as required under Section 44AA (2) and gets his accounts audited and furnishes a report of such audit under Section 44AB, and thereupon the assessing officer shall proceed to make an assessment of the total income or loss of the assessee under Section 143(3) and determine the sum payable by, or refundable to, the assessee.

Profits and Gains of the business of Operation of Aircraft (Section 44BBA)

The income of an NRI from the business of operation of aircraft is computed at a sum equal to 5% of the aggregate of the amounts paid or payable to him whether in India or outside

India on account of the carriage of passengers, livestock, mail or goods from any place in India.

Profits and Gains of Foreign Companies engaged in the business of Civil Construction, etc. in certain Turnkey Power Projects (Section 44BBB).

The income of a foreign company from the business of civil construction, or of erection of plant and machinery, or testing, or commissioning thereof in connection with turnkey power projects is computed at 10% of the amount paid or payable to it on account of such civil construction, erection, testing or commissioning. This used to be subject to the following conditions:

(i) The projects are approved by the Central Government on this behalf.

(ii) It is financed under any international aid program.

The Finance Act 2003 omitted the requirement of financing of such projects under any international aid program. It also proposes to provide that an assessee may claim lower profits and gains than specified, if he keeps and maintains such books of accounts and other documents as required under Section 44AA (2) and gets his accounts audited and furnishes a report of such audit under Section 44AB, and thereupon the assessing officer shall proceed to make an assessment of the total income or loss of the assessee under Section 143(3) and determine the sum payable by or refundable to the assessee.

Income of Non-Resident Sportsmen or Sports Associations (Section 115BBA)

Non-resident sportsmen, who are not Indian citizens, are charged a flat rate of 10% for earnings from participation in any game or sports (other than horse races) or from advertisements or from contribution of articles relating to games or sports in any newspapers, magazines or journals. Similarly, a non-resident sports association or institution is liable for tax at the rate of 10% on the guaranteed paid or payable to it in relation to any game (other than horse races) or sport played in India.

Special Provisions In Respect of Business of Prospecting for or Extraction of Mineral Oils (Section 293A)

The central bank has been authorized to grant by special notification reduction in rate or other modifications in respect of income tax in favor of the following class of persons:

(a) Persons with whom the Central Government has entered into agreements for participation in any business consisting of the prospecting for or extraction of production of mineral oils.

(b) Persons providing any service or faculties or supplying any ship, aircraft, machinery or plant (by way of sale or hire) in connection with any business consisting of the prospecting for or extraction or production of mineral oils carried on by the government or any persons specified by the government.

(c) Employees of persons referred to in (a) and (b) above.

In exercise of such power, the Central Government reduced the rate of tax in respect of income of a foreign company or other non-corporate non-resident of the nature mentioned at 55% (against the general rate of 65%). The Central Government is empowered to make a modification with regard to the status in which the aforesaid class of persons is to be assessed.

TAXATION OF INVESTMENT INCOME 8

NRIs are actively encouraged to invest in India. There are concessions given to them for doing so.

What are the rules regarding the taxation of investment income of NRIs and what are the concessions given?

Interest Income

Interest income received by or accruing in India to an NRI is taxable. Interest payable by the government or by any other person in respect of money used for business or a profession in India or for any source of income in India, is considered as income accrued in India.

Earlier some interest income was exempted from tax. The Finance Act 2005 has done away with this and replaced this deduction with an income-based deduction of Rs. 1,00,000 in order to help individuals to manage their businesses better.

Rate of Tax on Interest Income

Some non-residents are charged to tax of a fixed rate on the gross receipts without deduction of any expenses incidental to earning such income or deductions under Section 80.

(i) Non-residents* (* as provided by the Finance Act 2003) (not being a company) or foreign companies in respect of interest received from the government or an Indian concern on borrowing in foreign currency loans and income received from mutual fund units purchased in foreign currency (Section 115A) – tax rate of 20%.

(ii) Non-corporate, non-residents in respect of interest received from the Government or Indian concern on borrowing in foreign currency (Section 115A) – tax rate of 20%.

(iii) Offshore funds in respect of income from units purchased in foreign currency and long-term capital gains arising from the transfer of such units (Section 115AB) – tax rate of 10%.

(iv) Non-residents in respect of income from bonds and GDRs purchased on foreign currency and the long term capital gains arising from the transfer of such bonds or GDRs. (Section 115AC) – tax rate of 10%.

The Finance Act 2003 excluded dividends referred to in Section 115O from the purview of Section 115AC.

(v) Resident employees of an Indian company or its subsidiary company engaged in a specified, knowledge-based industry in respect of income by way of dividends from GDRs issued under ESOPs notified and also income by way of long-term capital gain arising from transfer of such GDRs. (Section 115ACA) – tax rate of 10%.

The Finance Act 2003 excluded dividends referred to in Section 115O from the purview of Section 115ACA.

(vi) Foreign institutional investors in respect of securities or capital gains arising from their transfer (the Finance Act 2003 excluded dividends on such securities from the preview, because of the amendment to Section 115O), listed in a recognized stock exchange in India in accordance with the Securities Contracts (Regulation) Act 1956 (other than units covered by Section115 AB) (Section 115AD) – tax rate of 20%.

(vii) Income from interest other than those specified above is charged to tax on a net income basis at the normal rate applicable to the taxpayer depending upon whether he is an individual, a company, or any other person.

Rates of Tax where there are Double Tax Avoidance Agreements

Based on double-tax avoidance agreements with different countries, income from interest derived by a person resident of the country with which such an agreement exists is chargeable at the agreed rates of tax mentioned above. If, however, in every case the rates in the agreement are higher, the taxpayer is entitled to be assessed at the general rates prescribed by the Income Tax Act.

Tax treatment of Dividend/Income from units

Dividend declared, distributed, or paid is fully taxable from the assessment year 2003-04. Dividend income, in case of certain non-residents, is taxed at a flat rate on gross receipts without deduction on any incidental expenses therefrom. For such non-resident persons, the rates applicable are: -

(i) Non-residents and foreign companies in respect of royalty and fees for technical services (Section 115A) – tax rate of 20%.

(ii) Non-corporate, non-residents in respect of interest on foreign currency loans or income from units of a mutual fund or the Unit Trust of India (UTI) purchased in foreign currency (Section 115 A) – tax rate of 20%.

The Finance Act 2003 excluded dividends referred in Section 115O from the purview of Section 115A.

(iii) Offshore funds (overseas financial organizations) in respect of units purchased in foreign currency and long-term capital gains arising from the transfer of such units. These are any fund institutions or bodies established under the laws of a country outside India which has entered into an arrangement for investment in India with any public sector bank or public financial institution or a notified mutual fund and such an arrangement is approved by the Central Government (Section 115AB) – tax rate of 10%.

(iv) Any NRI in respect of income from bonds and GDRs purchased in foreign currency and also any long-term capital gains arising on there transfer. (Section 115AC) – tax rate of 10%.

The Finance Act 2003 excluded dividends referred in Section115O from the purview of Section 115AC.

(v) Resident employees of a company engaged in specified, knowledge-based industries on income by way of dividends from GDRs issued in accordance with employee stock options, notified scheme and income arising by way of long-term capital gains on transfer of such GDRs. (Section 115ACA) – tax rate of 10%.

The Finance Act 2003 excluded dividends referred in Section115O from the purview of Section 115ACA.

(v) Foreign institutional investors:

(a) In respect of income from securities listed in a recognized stock exchange in India (other than units covered by Section115AB) – tax rate of 20%.

(b) Income by way of short-term capital gains arising from the transfer of such securities tax rate of 30%.

(c) Long-term capital gains arising therefrom – tax rate of 10%.

The Finance Act 2003 excluded dividends referred in Section115O from the purview of Section 115ACA.

Income from dividend declared before June 1, 1997 and after April 1, 2002 by an Indian company, or from units of notified mutual funds, or the Unit Trust of India, which is not specified above, is taxable on a net-income basis at the normal rate of tax.

The Finance Act 2003 exempted dividend income under Section 10(34) in the hands of the recipient, by levying a dividend distribution tax @ 12.5% (plus surcharge @ 2.5%) on the company at the time of the distribution of the dividend on all domestic companies under Section 115O. The Act inserted Section 10(33) to provide that any income arising from the transfer of a capital asset, being a unit of unit scheme, 1964 referred to the Unit Trust of India (Transfer of Undertaking and Repeal) Act 2002, where the transfer of asset takes place on or after the April 1, 2002, shall be exempted from tax.

The Act also inserted a Clause (35) to Section 10, to provide that any income by way of income received in respect of units from an administrator of the specified undertaking or the specified company or a mutual fund specified under Section 10(23D) shall be exempted.

Rates of Tax as per Double Tax Avoidance Agreements

Rates applicable to income from dividends are agreed to in the double-tax avoidance agreement entered into by India. The NRI is entitled to be assessed at the normal rate applicable him or the rate specified in the agreement with his country, whichever is favorable to him.

Tax Treatment of Capital Gains

There are some provisions applicable to NRIs on the computation of capital gains as well as the rates of taxation on these gains.

Special Provision for Computing Capital Gains from Transfer of Shares/Debentures

Capital gains made by NRIs from the sale of shares or debentures of Indian companies are computed by first converting the cost and the transfer consideration into the same foreign currency that was used to buy the shares/ debentures. The difference, which is the capital gain in foreign currency, is then re-converted into Indian rupees to determine the capital gain that is chargeable to tax. This is done to ensure that the amount of capital gain that is chargeable to tax is not influenced by exchange changes and only represents the increase in its value. The rate of conversion and re-conversion to be applied is the average of the telegraphic (TT) buying rate, for the cost of acquisition and the TT selling rate for the sale consideration on the respective dates (Rule 115A). For the conversion of the capital gains, the conversion rate will be the TT buying rate on the date of sale of the capital asset. This method of computation of capital gains is applicable in respect of capital gains accruing or arising from every reinvestment thereafter in shares or debentures of an Indian company.

To enable and facilitate the restructuring of business transfer of shares in Indian companies from one foreign company to another in a scheme of amalgamation, what would not be created? if two conditions are satisfied:

(1) At least 25% of the shareholders of the amalgamating company continue to be shareholders of the amalgamated company.

(2) Such transfer is not subject to capital gains tax in the country where the amalgamating company is incorporated.

Capital gains arising from the transfer of short-term capital assets are included in the total income and taxed at the normal rate applicable to the income of the person earning it. Capital gains arising out of the transfer of long-term capital assets in the hands of non-residents are, however, assessed at a flat rate of 10%.

Non-residents of certain categories are assessed at special concessional rates of tax in respect of capital gains arising from the transfer of certain specified assets. In these cases, the manner of compiling capital gains mentioned earlier is not to be applied. With regard to the following non-residents, capital gains tax will be as under:

(i) Overseas financial organizations with regard to long-term capital gains arising from the transfer of units purchased in foreign currency tax rate of 10%.

(ii) Any non-resident in respect of long-term capital gains from the transfer of bonds or shares of certain companies which are issued in accordance with a notified scheme and purchased by him in foreign currency tax rate of 10%.

(iii) Notified foreign institutional investors on capital gains from the transfer of securities listed in a recognized stock exchange:

(a) If the gain is short-term 30%

(b) If the gain is long-term 10%

The Finance Act 2003 inserted a new clause, Clause (36), to provide that any income arising from transfer of a long-term capital asset, being equity shares in a company listed on any recognized stock exchange in India and acquired on or after March 1, 2003 but before March 1, 2004, shall be exempted from tax.

The Finance Act 2004 abolished the capital gains tax payable on long-term gains arising from the sale of securities and shares. Short-term gains will be taxed at a flat rate of 10%.

Double Tax Avoidance Agreements

The jurisdiction of capital gains tax is governed by the double-tax avoidance agreement, if any, existing in the country to which the NRI belongs.

Exemption on Any Investment Income

The income the recipient receives net of tax payment from the Government of India or Indian concerned under an approved agreement, the tax paid by the payer of the income will not be considered as his income of the recipient and the requirement of grossing up will not apply (Section 10 (6B)).

Exemption from Filing Return of Income

If the income of non-residents governed by Sections 115A and 115AC consists only of the income from interest, dividend or income from units, and tax has been deducted at source, such persons do not need to file the return of income (which otherwise would have been required to file).

9

TAXATION OF INCOME OF NON-RESIDENTS FROM TRANSFER OF TECHNOLOGY, INCOME FROM ROYALTIES & FEES FOR TECHNICAL SERVICES

Royalty is the consideration for the transfer of rights in respect of or use of intellectual property, i.e. patents, inventions, etc. It includes consideration for giving information concerning technical, industrial, commercial or scientific knowledge, or skill. It does not matter whether the consideration is by way of a lump sum payment or in the term of recurring payments based on production or any other factor. It does not include income that arises from the transfer of the asset itself as that could be taxed as a 'capital gain'.

The fees for technical services constitute any consideration received for rendering any managerial, technical or consultancy services. It also includes consideration for providing services of a technical or personal nature as part of their service contract. It does not include consideration for any construction, assembly, mining or like projects undertaken by the recipient or consideration which would be the income of the recipient chargeable under the head 'salary' by virtue of an employer-employee relationship.

Royalty is taxable in the hands of NRIs if it is received in or accrued in India. Royalty paid by the government is considered accruing in India. If paid by any other person, it is the place of use of the intellectual property that governs the place of accrual. If the right property or information for which royalty is payable is used for business or profession in India, or for earning income in India, royalty is assumed to be accruing in India and is therefore chargeable to tax.

However, with regard to a lump-sum royalty payment made by a resident for transfer of right in respect of computer software supplied by a non-resident manufacturer, along with the supply of computers or computer-based equipment, such a lump sum payment is treated as the business income of the manufacturer.

Fees for technical services are taxable in the hands of NRIs if it is received in India or it accrues in India. The income would be considered as accruing in India if the fees are payable by the government. In respect of payments made by others, it is the place where the services are utilized that determines the accrual of income in India. If the services are utilized in business or profession in India or for earning income from any sources in India, the fees accrue in India.

Taxation

Royalty and fees for technical services in pursuance of agreements made are taxable at 20% of the gross receipt. Approvals are necessary from the government, unless they relate to a matter included in the industrial policy of the government. With regard to non-resident, non-corporate persons, this income is taxed at the normal rate on a net-income basis (after deduction of incidental expenses).

With regard to royalty for transfer of rights in respect of computer software permitted to be imported under OGL, a flat rate of 20% of gross receipts is applied.

Exemptions from Tax

The following income from royalty fees for technical services is exempted from tax.

(i) Royalty or fees for technical services are required free of tax under an agreement which relates to a matter included in the industrial policy and in accordance with such policy.

The requirements of grossing up applicable to net of tax payments will not apply to such income. (Section 10(6A)).

(ii) Fees for technical services and royalty (inserted by the Finance Act 2003) received by a notified foreign company based on an agreement for providing services in or outside India in projects connected with the security of India is exempted from tax (Section 10(6C)).

Double Tax Avoidance Agreements

Bilateral agreements entered into by India with foreign countries provide a concessional rate of tax on gross receipt basis in respect of this income. Taxpayers are entitled to be assessed at that rate or at the rate mentioned above (20%), whichever is beneficial to them.

The Finance Act 2003 inserted a new section, Section 44DA, in the Income Tax Act, relating to special provisions for computing income by way of royalties, etc., in case of NRIs. The section provides that the income by way of royalty for technical services received from the Government or an Indian concern in pursuance of an agreement made by a non-resident (not being a company) or a foreign company with Government to the Indian concern after March 31, 2003, where such non-resident (not being a company) or a foreign company carries on business in India through a permanent establishment situated therein, or performs professional services from a fixed place of profession situated therein, and the right, property or contract in respect of which the royalties or fees for technical services are paid is effectively connected with such permanent establishment or fixed place of profession, as the case may be, shall be computed under the head 'profits & gains of business or profession' in accordance with the provisions of the Income Tax Act. However, it is provided that no deduction shall be allowed in respect of any expenditure or allowance which is not wholly and exclusively incurred for the business of such permanent establishment or fixed place of profession in India; or in respect of amounts, if any, paid (otherwise than towards reimbursement of actual expenses) by the permanent establishment to its head office or any of its other offices.

The section also requires all non-residents (not being a company) or a foreign company to keep and maintain books of accounts and other documents in accordance with the provisions contained in Section 44AA and get the accounts audited by an accountant as defined in the explanation below Sub-section 288 and furnish along with the return of income, a report of such an audit duly signed and verified by such accountant.

SPECIAL INVESTMENT PROVISIONS 10

To attract investment by NRIs and Indian nationals living abroad, certain relief and exemptions have been provided. Chapter XIIA of the Income Tax Act contains special provision dealing with taxation of NRIs.

Joint Holdings of NRIs

Non-residents of Indian nationality/origin may invest in shares either singly or jointly with their close relatives, resident in India. RBI permits such joint holdings with repatriation benefits, provided:

(a) The investment is made by sending remittance from abroad or out of funds held in the overseas investors' NRE account or FCNR (B) deposit account.

(b) The first holder of shares is the non-resident who actually made the investment out of his funds; and

(c) The resident holder is closely related to the non-resident investor.

Remittance/repatriation of capital/dividend will be allowed to the non-resident investor, i.e. the first holder. In the event of the joint resident holder inheriting shares, he/she will not be entitled to any remittance/repatriation facilities. The special tax incentives provided in the act to non-residents of Indian origin are available only to them and not to the resident Indians. The following investment income arising to NRIs is totally exempted:

(1) The entire income accruing or arising to an NRI investing in units of the Unit Trust of India is free of income tax provided the units purchased by them are out of the amount remitted from abroad or from the NRE account.

(2) Income arising from investment in notified savings certificates obtained by NRIs is exempted from tax, provided the certificates are subscribed to in convertible foreign exchange remitted from a foreign country in accordance with the Foreign Exchange Management Act.

(3) Income from NRI bonds purchased by NRIs in foreign exchange is exempted from tax. This exemption continues to be available to an NRI even after he/she becomes a resident and is available also to the nominee or survivor of the NRI and to the donee (recipient) who receives a gift of such bonds from the NRI.

The income other than dividend and long-term capital gains derived from any foreign exchange asset by an NRI is charged to tax at the flat rate of 20%. Long-term capital gains arising on transfer of such assets are charged at the rate of 10%. In this instance, 'Foreign Exchange Asset' means any of the following assets acquired, purchased, or subscribed in convertible foreign exchange.

(a) Shares in an Indian company

(b) Debentures issued by a public limited company

(c) Deposits in a public limited company

(d) Securities of the Central Government

(e) Any other notified asset [No definition of 'Foreign Exchange Asset' in FEMA].

In computing the total income of such persons from any foreign exchange asset, no deduction is allowed in respect of any expenditure or allowance under any provision of the Act. Further, where an NRI has income only from foreign exchange assets or income by way of long-term capital gains arising in transfer of a foreign exchange asset, and the tax deductible at source has been deducted, he is not required to file a return of income.

The special provisions will continue to apply in relation to the investment income from foreign exchange assets, other than shares of an Indian company, even after the NRI becomes an Indian resident. If the NRI on becoming a resident wishes to be assessed under these provisions, he is required to file a declaration in writing along with the return of income. These special provisions will apply in relation to such income until the transfer or conversion of such assets into money.

An NRI may also elect not to be governed by these provisions for any assessment year by furnishing to the assessing officer the return of income for that assessment year and declaring that these provisions shall not apply to him for that assessment year. If he does so, then his total income and tax will be computed in accordance with the normal provisions of the act.

Any long-term capital gain arising to an NRI from the transfer of a foreign exchange asset, the net consideration of which is invested or deposited within a period of six months from the date of transfer in any specified asset mentioned at (a) to (e) of Para 11, 3 or in the National Saving Certificate VI or VII issues is dealt with as follows:

(a) If the cost of the new asset is not less than the net consideration in respect of the original foreign exchange asset, the whole of the capital gains will not be liable for tax.

(b) If the cost of the new asset is less than the net consideration in respect of the original foreign exchange asset, the proportionate amount of capital gain will be exempted from tax. The proportionate amount will be:

$$\text{capital gain} \times \frac{\text{cost of new assets}}{\text{net consideration of transfer}}$$

To simplify the procedure for tax deduction at source, NRIs wishing to remit sale proceeds of foreign exchange assets abroad or to non-resident (external) accounts can do so provided tax at 10% on the long-term capital gain is deducted by the authorized dealer.

11 DOUBLE TAX AVOIDANCE AGREEMENT

It is inequitable for individuals be taxed twice for the same income once in the country wherein the income has been earned and then again in India. This inequity has been realized and the Central Government is authorized under Section 90 of the Income Tax Act to enter into double-tax avoidance agreements (tax treaties) with other countries. The purpose of these agreements is to evolve an equitable basis for the allocation of the right to tax different types of income between source and residence status; hence, there would be tax neutrality in respect of transactions between residents and non-residents.

Tax treaties protect taxpayers against double taxation. They also prevent discrimination between the taxpayers in the international field and provide a reasonable element of legal and fiscal protection.

The treaties allocate jurisdiction between the source and residence country. Wherever both the countries have jurisdiction, the agreements usually prescribe the maximum rate of taxation in the source country, which is generally lower than the rate of tax under the domestic laws of that country. The double taxation in these cases is avoided by the residence country agreeing to give credit for tax paid in the source country, thereby, reducing tax payable in the residence country by the amount paid in the source country.

Let us assume that a resident in India has paid tax in Kenya on income earned at 32% on an income of the equivalent of Rs. 1,00,000. The tax he would have paid there would be Rs. 32,000. In India, as the tax rate is 30%, the tax credit given will be limited to 30% of Rs. 100,000 or Rs. 30,000. On the other hand, if the tax rate there (in Kenya) is 25%, the credit given will be Rs. 25,000. The rate, therefore, is that the credit will be limited to the lower of the tax payable in India (residence country) and the tax paid in the source country. With regard to non-residents, they can claim tax credits for amounts taxed in India, if the countries they reside in have tax treaties with India.

Tax agreements give the country of residence the right to tax interest, dividend, royalty, and fees for technical services. The source country also has the right to tax. The amount taxed in the source country has to be limited to the ratio prescribed in the agreement. The rate of tax is on gross receipts.

Regarding capital gains, gains arising from the transfer of immovable properties are taxed in the country where such properties are situated. Gains from the transfer of movable properties forming part of the business property of a 'permanent establishment' or the 'fixed base' are taxed in the country where such permanent establishment or the fixed base is located. There are other provisions for the taxation of capital gains arising from the transfer of shares. In several agreements, the right to tax is given to the state of which the company is resident. In some agreements, the country of residence of the shareholder has this right if the shareholding of the transferor is of a prescribed percentage.

The source country has the right to tax business income only if there is a permanent establishment or a fixed place of business there. Tax is levied on net income.

Income derived by rendering of professional services or other activities of independent character are taxable in the country of residence except when the person deriving income from such services has a field base in the country from where such services are performed. Such income is also taxable in the source country if the individual's stay exceeds 183 days in that financial year.

Income from dependent personal services, i.e. from employment, is taxed in the country of residence unless the employment is exercised in another state. Even if the employment is exercised in any other state, the remuneration will be taxed in the country of residence if:

(i) The recipient is present in the source state for a period not exceeding 183 days, and

(ii) The remuneration is paid by a person who is not a resident of that state, and

(iii) The remuneration is not borne by a permanent establishment or a fixed base.

The tax treaties would also provide for jurisdiction to tax director's fees, remuneration of persons in government service, payments received by students and apprentices, income of entertainers and athletes, pensions and social security payments, and other incomes.

Double-tax avoidance agreements also contain clauses for non-discrimination of the nationals of a contracting state in the other state vis-a-vis the nationals of that other state.

Provisions also exist for mutual agreements procedures which authorize the competent authorities of the two states to resolve any dispute that may arise in the matter of taxation without going through the normal process of appeals, etc. provided under the domestic law.

Some agreements have a clause providing for this exchange of information between the two contracting states, which may be necessary for carrying out the provisions of the agreement or for effective implementation of domestic laws concerning taxes covered by the tax treaty. Information about residents getting payments in other contracting states necessary to be known for proper assessments of total income of such individuals are thus facilitated by such agreements.

It may sometimes happen that due to a reduction in tax rates under domestic law taking place after coming into existence of the treaty, the domestic rates become more favorable to non-residents. Since the objective of tax treaties is to benefit non-residents, they have, under such circumstances, the option to be assessed either as per the provisions of the treaty or the domestic law of the land.

To avoid any demand or refund consequent to assessment and to facilitate the process of assessment, it has been provided that tax shall be deducted at source, out of payments, to non-residents at the same rate at which the particular income to made taxable under the tax treaties.

Exhibit I: Some countries with which India has Double Tax Avoidance Agreements

1. Australia
2. Austria
3. Bangladesh
4. Belarus
5. Belgium
6. Brazil
7. Bulgaria
8. Canada
9. China
10. Cyprus
11. Czech Republic
12. Denmark
13. Germany
14. Finland
15. France
16. Greece
17. Hungary
18. Indonesia
19. Ireland
20. Israel

21. Italy
22. Japan
23. Jordan
24. Kazakhstan
25. Kenya
26. Korea
27. Libya
28. Kyrgyz Republic
29. Malaysia
30. Malta
31. Mongolia
32. Mauritius
33. Morocco
34. Namibia
35. Nepal
36. Netherlands
37. New Zealand
38. Norway
39. Oman
40. Philippines
41. Poland
42. Portuguese Republic
43. Qatar
44. Romania
45. Russian Federation
46. Singapore
47. South Africa
48. Spain
49. Sri Lanka
50. Sweden

51. Swiss
52. Syria
53. Tanzania
54. Thailand
55. Trinidad & Tobago
56. Turkey
57. Turkmenistan
58. UAE
59. UAR (United Arab Republic Egypt)
60. UK
61. Ukraine
62. US
63. Uzbekistan
64. Vietnam
65. Zambia

Please note: This is not a complete list, and readers are advised to check with a tax attorney or consultant for up-to-date information.

12

FILING RETURNS AND ASSESSMENTS

Filing Returns

If an NRI's income is below Rs. 1,10,000 for the financial year, he does not need to file a return. He also does nct need to file a return if his income is only investment income and he is paying income tax at the uniform rate of 20%. However, an NRI may have other income or he may opt for a normal assessment procedure to secure a lower incidence of income tax. Under such cases where an NRI chooses to file an Income Tax Return or where he is required to file an Income Tax Return, he should know the assessment procedure so that he can file his return on time and, if appropriate, claim refund of income tax.

If the NRI has income assessable to tax, he is required under Section 139 (1) of the Income Tax Act to file his return in Form No. 2 or Form No. 2D or Form No. 3 (as may be applicable) before June 30. In case of business income, the return can be filed by August 31 or October 31 (in the case of tax audit or in the case of a working partner whose accounts are subject to a tax audit). In case of belated returns, penal interest at 15% per annum will be levied.

The return under Section 139 (1) or 139 (2) can be signed by the NRI himself or by some person duly authorized by him on this behalf where the NRI is absent from India. In some cases, the return can also be filed by the agent of the NRI (known as a representative).

An assessing officer (Income Tax Officer) can require an NRI who, in his opinion, had taxable income during the relevant previous year to submit a return of income within 30 days of the receipt of such notice. Penal interest will be charged by the assessing officer for delay in filing the return.

Self-assessment tax under the provisions of Section 140A must be paid before filing the return of income, and a copy of the challan for the self-assessment tax must be enclosed with the return. All the required statements, challans, certificates, etc. regarding the income of the NRI must be filed with the return of income.

When, in a business carried on between a resident and a non-resident, the course of business is arranged in a manner that the business produced to the resident generates either no profits or less than the ordinary profits, the assessing officer could determine the profits which may reasonably be deemed to have been derived therefrom. This problem arises where the dealings between the two are not at arms' length and an arrangement through transfer pricing is resorted to reduce the profit taxable in India. In such cases, Chapter X procedure dealing with transfer pricing has to be followed in arriving at the transfer price.

Assessment of Non-Residents through Agents (Section 163)

A non-resident may be assessed to tax in India either directly or through agents. A person in India who may be treated as an 'agent' of a non-resident is:

(i) An employee of the non-resident.

(ii) Any person who has any business connection with the non-resident.

Any person from or through whom the non-resident is in receipt of any income.

Any person who is a trustee of the non-resident.

Any person who has acquired a capital asset in India from the non-resident.

An NRI may also appoint an authorized representative to act as his agent. Such an agent can file returns, claim refunds and deal with income tax matters.

A broker in India who has independent dealings with a non-resident broker acting on behalf of a non-resident principal is, however, not treated, as an agent of the non-resident, if the transactions between the two brokers are carried on in the ordinary course of their business.

Refund

Where the amount of income tax deductible from the income of an NRI, or the amount of advance tax, or any other tax paid by him or treated as paid by him, or on his behalf for any assessment year exceeds the amount by which he is properly chargeable under the Income Tax Act for that year, he would be entitled to a refund of the excess income tax. Every claim for refund has to be made in the prescribed Form No. 30 obtainable from any Income Tax Office/Officer. A claim must be made within one year from the last date of the assessment year. Interest at 0.67% per month from April 1 of the assessment year is payable on the amount of the refund.

Return and Scrutiny

On receipt of a return, the Income Tax Officer may send an intimation enquiring whether any modifications are required. Nowadays, 97% of cases are accepted without scrutiny. In such cases, the acknowledgement slip serves the purpose of an assessment order under Section 143 (1). The returns of NRIs are excluded from detailed scrutiny if the total income declared is at least 30% more than the total income for the previous year and does not exceed Rs. 5 lakh. The Finance Act 1999 has, from June 1, 1999 taken away the power of the assessing officer to make adjustments while making a provisional assessment under Section 143 (1) of the Income Tax Act.

Regular Assessment after Personal Hearing

If the assessing officer wishes to verify the correctness of the return by requiring the presence of the assessee or the production of evidence for this purpose, the officer must serve the assessee with a notice for personal hearing or production of evidence in support of the return under Section 143 (2) of the Income Tax Act. This occurs when a case is selected for detailed scrutiny. In such instances the assessing officer has to make an assessment under Section 143 (3) of the Income Tax Act. A compulsory audit may be required if the turnover exceeds Rs. 40 lakh.

Ex-Parte Assessment

Where a Non-Resident Indian fails to file a return under Section 139 (2) of the Income Tax Act or does not comply with the provisions of Section 142 (1) of the Act regarding the production of accounts or a notice under Section 143 (2) of the Act regarding the production of income, the assessing officer can make an assessment of the total income of the NRI to the best of his judgment and determine the sum payable or refundable to him on the basis of such assessment.

Reassessment or Additional Assessment in Case of Income Escaping Assessment

Where the income tax payable/chargeable has been under assessed or where the income has been assessed at too low a rate or where excessive relief is granted, the assessing officer may reassess such income or re-compute the loss for the period. If the assessing officer feels that such assessment/reassessment is due to omission or failure of the NRI to disclose all the facts fully, the assessing officer can issue a notice under Section 147(a)/148 within four to six years (depending on the quantum of income involved).

Special Procedure for Assessment of Income of an NRI from Foreign Exchange Assets

There are certain types of investment incomes of a Non-Resident Indian where there is a special procedure of assessment. Under this procedure, an NRI does not need to pay income tax in India at the slab rates of income tax but can pay at a special ad hoc rate of 20% (10% on long-term capital gains) on the entire income without any deduction of any type (as permitted under various provisions of the Income Tax Act). Thus, there is no risk of the NRI paying tax at 30% (the rate applicable to a resident Indian on income in excess of Rs. 1.5 lakh). This is as per the provisions of Sections 115C and 115I of the Income Tax Act 1961.

Section 115D states that no deduction of any expenditure or allowance will be allowed in computing the investment income of an NRI. Where the NRI's gross total income consists only of investment income or income by way of long-term capital gains or both, no deduction will be allowed under Chapter VI A of the Income Tax Act. Additionally nothing contained in the second proviso of Section 48 would apply to the capital gains of NRIs. Where the gross total income of an NRI includes any income of the kind mentioned above, the total income is reduced by the amount of such income and if any deductions under Chapter VIA of the Income Tax Act are to be allowed, they will be allowed as if the gross total income so reduced is the gross total income of the assessee.

It must be noted that only income of certain selected assets are eligible for the special concession. These are known as 'foreign exchange assets'. They are defined in Section 115 (b) of the Income Tax Act as "any specified asset, which the assessee has acquired or subscribed in a convertible foreign exchange". Investment income means any income derived from foreign exchange assets. Section 115 (f) of the Income Tax Act defines specific assets as:

- Shares in an Indian company
- Debentures issued by an Indian company, which is not a private company as defined in the Companies Act 1956
- Deposits with an Indian company, which is not a private company
- Any security of the Central Government

Such other assets as the Central Government may specify

on this behalf by notification in the official gazette.

The levy of income tax is stated in Section 115E. If the total income of an NRI consists only of investment income or income from long-term capital assets, then tax would be payable on the total income at the rate of 10%.

Section 115F of the Income Tax Act provides for complete exemption of long-term capital gains on the transfer of foreign exchange assets in certain cases. Where an NRI has a long-term capital gain from the transfer of a foreign exchange asset and the NRI has, within a period of six months from the date of such transfer, deposited the whole or any part of the net consideration in any specified asset or in an account referred to in Section 10(4) or in Savings Certificates (Section 10 (4B)), then no tax is payable. If the net consideration is invested in the purchase of a specified asset, no tax is payable on the long-term gain. However, if only a portion of the net consideration is invested, income tax is payable on the amount not invested.

It is provided in Sub-section 2 of Section 115F of the Income Tax Act that where the net asset is transferred or converted into money within a period of three years from the date of its acquisition, the amount of capital gains arising from the transfer of the original assets not so charged under Section 45, will be deemed to be income chargeable under the head 'capital gains' relating to the long-term asset of the previous year in which the new asset is transferred or converted into money. In short, long-term capital gains can be free of income tax if they are invested in specified assets.

An NRI who has income from foreign exchange assets only does not need to file a return under Section 115G if both the following conditions are met:

- His total income during the previous year which is assessable under the Income Tax Act consisted only of investment income or income by way of long-term capital gains or both.
- The tax deductible at source under the provisions of

Chapter XVII has been deducted from such income.

Under Section 115H, an NRI who becomes a resident in respect of the total income of any subsequent year can continue to be assessable to income tax at 20%. For this, he has to exercise his option (Chapter XII A) by furnishing to the assessing officer a declaration in writing along with his return of income under Section 139 for the assessment which he is assessable to the effect that the provisions of Chapter XII A would continue to apply to him with regard to investment in shares of a limited company. However, the income arising from investments in shares of a limited company will not get this tax concession when the NRI becomes a resident.

It must be noted that under Chapter XIIA, the levy of a uniform rate of 20% is not compulsory and the NRI must so elect to choose. The NRI will not elect if he finds that the levy at the normal rates of tax would translate to a lower income tax liability than the uniform rate of 20%. This would happen when the total income is over Rs. 2 lakh. In such a case, the NRI would need to furnish to the assessing officer a return of income for the relevant year declaring that the provisions of Chapter XIIA would not be applicable to him for that assessment year.

An NRI must calculate his income before deciding whether to avail of the provisions of Chapter XIIA or not.

Completion of Assessment and Payment of Tax

The time limit of a regular assessment under Section 143 or 144 is a period of two years from the end of the assessment year in which the income was first assessable. Income tax and other dues must be paid within the time mentioned in the demand notice. Normally, a period of 30 days is allowed to an assessee for making the payment of income tax and other dues as mentioned in the notice of demand. If the entire tax cannot be paid at one time, an NRI can make an application to permit payment of tax in suitable installments. Interest at a specified percentage per month is normally required to be paid for the period of the belated payment.

Penal Interest

Under Section 234A of the Income Tax Act, penal interest at 1.25% per month is payable on the belated submission of the Income Tax Return if an NRI is required to voluntarily submit it. Similarly, if he does not submit the return within 30 days of receiving a notice from the assessing officer requiring him to do so, penal interest is charged.

On the other hand, if the refund of tax is not paid by the tax authorities, interest at 0.67% per month is payable by the Central Government under Section 244A of the Income Tax Act. If income has been concealed, the minimum penalty to be levied under Section 271(1) (c) is equal to the income tax sought to be evaded. With regard to non-payment of tax, a penalty can be levied under Section 221 which should not exceed 100% of the arrears of income tax.

Deduction of Tax at Source and Payment of Advance Tax

Various incomes are subject to tax at source. Advance tax is payable on the total income. Credit is given for this through regular assessment.

Where advance tax is payable, the assessee computes the advance tax payable on his current income at the rate in force in the financial year and deposits it. No estimate needs to be filed.

Under Section 211 of the Income Tax Act, up to 30%, 60%, and 100% of the tax payable in the year is payable in advance by September 15, December 15, and March 15, respectively. Any payment before March 31 will be treated as advance tax. Interest on default in the payment of advance tax is payable at 15% per annum (Section 234B), Under Section 234C, interest is charged at 1.25% per month in case of deferment of installments of advance tax or at 1.25% per month on the shortfall in the payment of tax till March 15.

Remedies By Way of Appeal

The right of appeal against an order is given to the taxpayer and not the income tax department. Against an order of assessment or refund, the NRI can file an appeal in Form 35 to the Commissioner of Income Tax (CIT) (Appeals) within 30 days. The minimum and maximum filing fees are Rs. 250 and Rs. 1,000 respectively. The CIT (Appeals) will then fix a hearing. Normally, an order will be passed in one year. A further appeal against the order of CIT (Appeals) can be made to the Income Tax Appellate Tribunal (ITAT). Such an appeal is to be filed in Form 36. The period of limitation for appeal is 60 days from the date the order is communicated to the assessee or CIT. The filing fee is a minimum of Rs. 500 or a maximum of Rs. 10,000. The order by the tribunal is passed normally within four years and is final on questions of fact. Against a tribunal decision, a direct appeal can be made to the High Court within 60 days and against a High Court decision to the Supreme Court.

Rectification

A mistake can be rectified by the concerned authority within four years. No rectification, which is adverse to the assessee can be made without giving a proper notice to the assessee.

Tax Clearance Certificate before Departure from India

Earlier, any individual leaving India had to take a tax clearance certificate from the Income Tax Department. However, recently this requirement of a tax clearance certificate has been done away with and this clearance is now required only for persons notified by the government.

Advance Rulings

To avoid disputes in the assessment of non-residents, there is a scheme of advance ruling. This scheme enables non-residents to obtain, in advance, a binding ruling from Income Tex authority for advance ruling on issues which could arise in determining their tax liabilities.

Under Section 245Q of the Income Tax Act, an NRI can

obtain an advance ruling about his tax liability in India by filing an application before the authority for advance rulings accompanied with a fee of Rs. 2,500. The ruling is binding on the NRI and the Income Tax Department. It was decided in 237 ITR 827 (1999) that the applicant must be a non-resident in the previous year preceding the financial year in which the application is filed.

Thus, time-consuming and expensive appeals can be avoided. Such issues may relate to transactions undertaken or proposed to be undertaken by the non-resident applicant. Such an advance ruling:

(1) Helps non-residents in planning their income tax affairs well in advance

(2) Helps in avoiding long-drawn and expensive litigation.

The advance ruling can be sought on any question of law or fact in relation to a transaction, which has been undertaken or is proposed to be undertaken by the non-resident applicant.

However, an advance ruling cannot be sought where the question:

(i) Is already pending in the case of the applicant before any income tax authority, the Appellate Tribunal or any court; or

(ii) Involves determination of fair market, value of any property; or

(iii) Relates to a transaction, which is designed prima facie for avoidance of income tax.

Advance ruling can be procured by the NRI by making an application (Form 34C). A fee has to be paid while making the application. The ruling has to be made within six months from the date of the application.

Advance rulings would be binding in respect of the transaction:

(a) On the commissioner and the income tax authorities subordinate to him in respect of the applicant; and

(b) On the applicant who had sought it.

WEALTH TAX 13

NRIs, Indians resident in India, HUFs, and certain companies are required to pay wealth tax on the assets they own on March 31 of the previous year. Thus, in the assessment year 2007-2008, an individual would have to pay wealth tax on his assets as on March 31, 2007.

Wealth tax is payable where the net wealth of taxable assets on a valuation date exceeds Rs. 15 lakh. This amount of Rs. 15 lakh is after considering certain assets that are exempted. Under the provisions of Section 3 of the Wealth Tax Act, wealth tax is chargeable at the flat rate of 1% of the amount by which the net wealth exceeds Rs. 15 lakh. The expression 'net wealth' refers to assets only. 'Assets' under Section 2(2) of the Wealth Tax Act means the following nonproductive assets on which wealth tax is levied.

1. Guest houses and any residential building or land appurtenance there to or a farmhouse situated within 25 kilometers from the local limits of any municipality. It does not include a house meant exclusively for residential purposes and is allotted to an employee/officer/director who has whole-time employment with a gross salary of less than Rs. 5 lakh. Any house for residential or commercial purposes which form part of stock in trade is not liable for wealth tax. Similarly, any house occupied for the purpose of any business or profession is exempted from wealth tax.
2. Motor cars other than used in the business and/or being run on hire or held as stock in trade.
3. Jewelry, furniture, utensils or any other articles made fully or partially of gold, silver, platinum, or other precious metals.
4. Yachts, boats, and aircraft not used for commercial purposes.

5. Urban land: Urban land means any land situated in any area comprised within the jurisdiction of the Municipality or a Cantonment Board which has a population of not less than 10,000 or any land situated within eight kilometers from the local limits of any municipality or cantonment board. Urban land, however, does not include land on which building construction is not permissible, or land occupied by any building which has been constructed with the approval of the appropriate authority, or any unused land held by the assessee for industrial purposes for a period of two years from the date of its acquisition by him, or any land held by the assessee as stock in trade for a period of 10 years from the date of its acquisition.
6. Cash in hand in excess of Rs. 50,000 for individuals and HUFs.

Assets not covered above are not liable for wealth tax.

Specific Exemptions

There are specific exemptions from wealth tax under Section 5 of the Wealth Tax Act.

1. Any property held by the tax-payer under trust or any other legal obligation for any practical purposes of charitable or religious nature in India.
2. The interest of the assessee in the coparcenary property (joint inheritance) of any HUF of which he is a member.
3. One house or part of a house or any plot of land not exceeding 500 sq. meters in area.
4. Jewelry in the possession of a former ruler.
5. One building in the occupation of a former ruler.
6. Assets acquired by an NRI within one year of his returning to India for permanent settlement. These assets must be acquired out of money brought into the country. This exemption is for a period of seven years commencing on the assessment year after his return.

Clubbing with Parents

Under Section 4 of the Wealth Tax Act, the wealth of a minor child is clubbed with the wealth of that parent whose wealth is higher. If, however, the parents are divorced, the clubbing of the net wealth of the child will be with that parent who maintains the minor child in the assessment year.

Assets outside India

Section 6 of the Wealth Tax Act provides that in computing the net wealth tax of an individual who is not a resident of India, or resident but not ordinarily resident, the value of assets and debts located outside India and the value of the assets in India represented by loans or debts owing to the assessee where the interest on these is not to be included in the total income of the individual. In short, an NRI is liable for wealth tax for non-productive Indian assets only.

Assessment Procedure

The assessment procedure is broadly in the same pattern as under the Income Tax Act. An NRI is liable for wealth tax only when the net taxable wealth in India exceeds Rs. 15 lakh.

The return of net wealth is to be filed on or before the date of voluntary submission of the income tax return.

The rate of wealth tax is 1% of the net wealth in excess of Rs. 15 lakh.

14 CAPITAL GAINS

A capital gain arises from the sale of a capital asset.

A short-term capital asset is a capital asset held for 36 months or less immediately preceding the date of transfer. This is reduced to 12 months or less in respect of company shares and units of approved mutual funds including units of the Unit Trust of India. In this regard, the cost of bonus shares is to be taken as nil. The cost of rights shares is to be at their issue price and the purchase of the right to apply for rights at the price paid. Any long-term capital gain is chargeable to tax at a 20% rate.

However, where the transferred long-term capital asset is in the nature of listed securities, or units of UTI, or another mutual fund, the gain arising from the transfer of such securities or units shall be eligible to tax at the rate of 10% on such long-term capital gains computed without the benefit of indexation or at the rate of 20% on such long-term capital gain computed after availing of the benefit of indexation, which ever is more beneficial to the assessee.

The Finance Act 2003, inserted Section 10(33) to provide that any income arising from the transfer of a capital asset, being a unit of unit scheme, 1964 referred to the Unit Trust of India (Transfer of Undertaking and Repeal) Act 2002, where the transfer of asset takes place on or after the April 1, 2002, shall be exempted from tax.

Long-term capital gains arising on the sale of foreign exchange assets are exempted from tax under Section 115F if the net sale consideration is reinvested in shares, debentures, or bank deposits within six months from the date of sale. If the reinvestment is less than the capital gains, proportional exemption is available. The new asset has to have a lock-in of three years. If it is transferred or encashed before three years, the income chargeable to long-term capital gains saved shall be deemed to be the income chargeable to long-term capital gains tax during the year when the new asset was sold.

The gains chargeable to tax arising from the sale of shares and investments are arrived at by reducing the cost of acquisition from the net sale proceeds. The tax charged on long- term capital gains by NRIs is 10%. The tax on short-term gains is at the normal rate.

The Finance Act 2003 inserted a new section, Section 10(36), to provide that any income arising from transfer of a long-term capital asset, being equity shares in a company listed on any recognized stock exchange in India and acquired on or after March 1, 2003 but before March 1, 2004, shall be exempted from tax.

The Finance Bill 2007 proposes to widen the scope of capital assets. A capital asset is defined as property of any kind held by an assessee, whether or not connected with his business or procession. Personal effects held for personal use by the assessee or any members of his/her family dependant on him/her are excluded from the ambit of definition of capital asset. Presently, the only asset which is in the nature of personal effects but is included in the definition of capital assets is jewelry.

To widen the scope of capital assets, the Finance Bill 2007 proposes to exclude from the meaning of personal effects archaeological collections, drawings, paintings, sculptures, or any work of art. Transfer of such personal effects will attract capital gains tax.

This amendment will be with effect from April 1, 2008 and will apply in relation to assessment year 2008-09 and subsequent years.

Cost inflation index

The cost of acquisition is to be increased by the cost inflation index, which is as follows:

Financial Year	Inflation Index	Financial Year	Inflation Index
1981-82	100	1993-94	244
1982-83	109	1994-95	259
1983-84	116	1995-96	281
1984-85	125	1996-97	305
1985-86	133	1997-98	331
1986-87	140	1998-99	351
1987-88	150	1999-00	389
1988-89	161	2000-01	406
1989-90	172	2001-02	426
1990-91	182	2002-03	447
1991-92	199	2003-04	463
1992-93	223	2004-05	480
2005-06	497	2006-07	519

The benefit of indexation shall not be allowed in the computation of long-term capital gain arising from the transfer of a long-term capital asset being bonds or debentures other than capital-indexed bonds issued by the Government of India. Also, indexation benefit is not available in computing the capital gains arising from the transfer of shares held in an Indian company by a non-resident acquired out of convertible foreign exchange.

Section 70 provides that loss from any source under any head of income, other than 'capital gains', can be set off against income from any head of income from any other source under the same head. As regards loss under the head 'capital gains', the treatment differs between short-term capital loss and long-term capital loss. Although short-term capital loss can be set off against either short-term capital gain or long-term capital gain, a long-term capital loss can be set off only against long-term capital gain.

Section 74 enabling the carry forward and set-off of the loss under the head 'capital gains' is modified by the Finance Act 2002 to provide for different treatment in case of long-term capital loss as against short-term capital loss. While short-term capital loss can be carried forward and set off against any income assessable under the head 'capital gains', the long-term capital loss can be set off only against long-term capital gain within a period of eight assessment years.

Special Provisions for Non-Residents

For a non-resident assessee, capital gains arising from transfer of capital asset being the shares or debentures of an Indian company shall be computed by converting cost of acquisition, expenses incurred for the transfer, and sale consideration into the same foreign currency as was utilized for the purchase of shares and debentures as indicated in Table 1. The capital gain so computed in such foreign currency shall be re-converted into Indian currency for the purpose of further computation as per the first proviso to Section 48 and Rule 115A.

Table 1:

Computation of gains

Items Converted/Reconverted	Rate of Conversion/Re-conversion
Cost of acquisition	The average of the TT selling and buying rate on the date of the transfer.
Expenses incurred for transfer	The average of the TT selling and buying rate on the date of the transfer.
Sale consideration	The average of the TT

	selling and buying rate on the date of the transfer.
Capital gains (Re-conversion)	The TT buying rate on the date of the transfer.

The conversion and re-conversion shall be made on the basis of the rate of exchange adopted by the State Bank of India.

The aforesaid manner of computation of capital gains shall be applicable in respect of capital gains arising from every reinvestment thereafter in the shares or debentures of an Indian company on the sale of such assets.

Also, the benefit of indexation will not be available in the computation of capital gains.

FOREIGN INVESTMENTS IN INDIA 15

Foreign Investments in India attract the provisions of Section 6 of the Foreign Exchange Management Act (FEMA) 1999 and is subject to the Regulations issued by RBI under FEMA, 1999.

An Indian entity cannot issue any security to a person resident outside India or record in its books any transfer of security from or to such person except as provided in the Act or Rules or Regulations or with the specific permission of RBI.

Prohibition on investment into India

No person resident outside India can invest in a company or a partnership firm, or a proprietary concern or any entity, whether incorporated or not, which is engaged or proposes to engage in the following activities:

(i) Business of chit fund, or

(ii) Nidhi Company, or

(iii) Agricultural or plantation activities or

(iv) Real estate business, or construction of farm houses

(v) Trading in Transferable Development Rights (TDRs).

It is clarified that Real Estate Business does not include development in townships, construction of residential/ commercial premises, roads or bridges. In addition to the above activities, Foreign Direct Investment (FDI) is also prohibited in certain activities.

Permitted Investments in India

In other cases, investments can be made either with the specific prior approval of the Government of India, the Secretariat for Industrial Assistance/Foreign Investment Promotion Board (SIA/FIPB) or under the Automatic Route.

The Automatic Route is not open in the following cases and as such requires specific approval of FIPB i.e.:

(i) Where the non-resident investors who have/had a previous financial/technical/ trademark collaboration in an existing domestic company engaged in the same or allied activity

(ii) If the activity or manufacturing item of the issuer company requires an Industrial License under the provisions of the Industries (Development and Regulation) Act, 1951 or under the locational policy notified by Government of India under the Industrial Policy Resolution, 1991

(iii) The investment is sought in excess of the prescribed sectoral limits.

While the nature of investment activities have been prescribed in the FEMA Regulations, the scope of these activities especially regarding the investments by non-residents under the Government approval route have been detailed in the Government Manual on Investing in India, Foreign Direct Investment, Policy & Procedures. This is a document available in the public domain and can be downloaded from the website of DIPP, Ministry of Commerce and Industry.

Eligibility for Investing in India

A person resident outside India (other than a citizen of Pakistan or Bangladesh) or an incorporated entity outside India, (other than an entity incorporated in Bangladesh or Pakistan) has the general permission to purchase shares or convertible debentures or preference shares of an Indian company subject to certain terms and conditions

Nature of Investments

Indian companies have general permission to issue equity/ preference/convertible preference shares and convertible debentures subject to certain conditions.

Investment in a trading company incorporated in India is permitted under Automatic Route with FDI up to 51% provided the Indian company is primarily engaged in export activities, and the undertaking is an export house/trading house/super trading house/star trading house. The Government also permits certain trading activities under the FIPB route.

A company which is a small scale industrial unit and which is not engaged in any activity or in manufacture of items that are not permitted may issue shares or convertible debentures to a non-resident, to the extent of 24% of its paid-up capital. Such a company may issue shares in excess of 24% of its paid-up capital if:

a) It has given up its small scale status,

b) It is not engaged or does not propose to engage in manufacture of items reserved for small scale sector, and

c) It complies with the ceilings specified in CBDT (Central Bureau of Direct taxes).

An Export Oriented Unit (EOU), or a unit in a Free Trade Zone, or in an Export Processing Zone, or in a Software Technology Park, or in an Electronic Hardware Technology Park may issue shares or convertible debentures to a person resident outside India in excess of 24% provided it conforms to the ceilings specified in Annexure B to Notification No. 94 as annexed at Annex-2.

FDI in Asset Reconstruction Companies (ARCs)

Persons/entities resident outside India (other than Foreign Institutional Investors (FIIs)), eligible under the FDI Scheme for investing in India are permitted to invest in the equity capital of ARCs registered with RBI. Such investments have to be strictly in the nature of FDI and investments by FIIs are not permitted. Automatic Route is not available for such investments. The applications are considered by FIPB subject to the following conditions:

(a) Maximum foreign equity shall not exceed 49% of the paid-up equity capital of the ARC.

(b) Where investment by any individual entity exceeds 10% of the paid-up equity capital, the ARC should comply with the provisions of Section 3 (3) (f) of Securitization and Reconstruction of Financial Assets and Enforcement of Security Interest Act, 2002 (SARFAESI Act or Securitisation Act), which states that a sponsor, shall not be a holding company of the securitization company or reconstruction company, as the case may be, or, does not otherwise hold any controlling interest in such securitization company or reconstruction company, for the purpose of obtaining registration from RBI.

General permission has been granted to FIIs registered with the Securities and Exchange Board of India (SEBI) to invest in Security Receipts (SRs) issued by ARCs registered with RBI. FIIs can invest up to 49% of each tranche of scheme of SRs subject to the condition that investment of a single FII in each tranche of scheme of SRs shall not exceed 10% of the issue.

General Permissions granted under the Regulations

Issue of Rights/Bonus shares

General permission is also available to Indian companies to issue right/bonus shares to existing non-resident share-holders, subject to adherence to sectoral cap and consequential offer on right basis is made at a price not lower than that at which offer is made to the resident shareholder. As clarified in terms of AP (DIR Series) Circular No 14 dated September 16, 2003, entitlement of rights shares is not automatically available to investors who have been allotted such shares as Overseas Corporate Bodies (OCBs). Such issuing companies would have to seek specific permission from RBI, and the Foreign Exchange Department, Foreign Investment Division, Central Office, Mumbai, for issue of shares on right basis to erstwhile OCBs. However, bonus shares can be issued to OCBs.

Existing non-resident shareholders are allowed to apply for issue of additional equity shares or preference shares or convertible debentures over and above their rights entitlements and the investee company can allot the same subject to the condition that the overall issue of shares to non-residents in the total paid-up capital of the company does not exceed the sectoral cap.

Acquisition of Shares under Scheme of Amalgamation/ Merger

Where a scheme of merger or amalgamation of two or more Indian companies has been approved by a court in India, the transferee company may issue shares to the shareholders of the transferor company, resident outside India, subject to ensuring that the percentage of shareholding of persons resident outside India in the transferee or new company does not exceed the percentage specified in the approval granted by the Central Government or RBI. The transferor company or the transferee or new company should not be engaged in activities prohibited in terms of the FDI policy viz agriculture, plantation or real estate business, or trading in TDRs etc.

Issue of Shares under ESOP

A company may issue shares under ESOP, to its employees or employees of its joint venture or wholly owned subsidiary abroad who are resident outside India, other than citizens of Pakistan, directly or through a Trust subject to the condition that the scheme has been drawn in terms of relevant regulations issued by SEBI, and face value of the shares to be allotted under the scheme to the non-resident employees does not exceed 5% of the paid-up capital of the issuing company. The issuing company is required to report the details and submit certificate stipulated to RBI, within 30 days from the date of issue of shares.

Advance Reporting

An Indian company issuing shares or convertible debentures as bonus, rights, or as stock options to persons resident outside India directly or on amalgamation/merger with an existing Indian company in accordance with these Regulations, should submit to RBI the details of advance remittance, not later than 30 days from the date of receipt of the amount of consideration, giving details regarding:

- Name and address of the foreign investors
- Date of receipt of funds and their rupee equivalent
- Name and address of the authorized dealer through whom the funds have been received, and
- Details of Government approval, if any.

Reporting Issue of Shares

After issue of shares the Indian company has to file a report in Form FC-GPR not later than 30 days from the date of issue of shares with the Regional Office of RBI under whose jurisdiction the registered office of the company is situated.

Issue of shares by Indian companies under ADR/GDR

An Indian corporate can raise foreign currency resources abroad through the issue of American Depository Receipts (ADRs) or Global Depository Receipts (GDRs). Regulation 4 of Schedule I of FEMA Notification no. 20 allows an Indian company to issue its rupee-denominated shares to a person resident outside India being a depository for the purpose of issuing GDRs and/or ADRs, subject to the conditions that:

- the ADRs/GDRs are issued in accordance with the Scheme for issue of Foreign Currency Convertible Bonds and Ordinary Shares (Through Depository Receipt Mechanism) Scheme, 1993 and guidelines issued by the Central Government thereunder from time to time
- The Indian company issuing such shares has an approval from the Ministry of Finance, Government of India to issue such ADRs and/or GDRs or is eligible to issue ADRs/GDRs in terms of the relevant scheme in force or notification issued by the Ministry of Finance, and
- Is not otherwise ineligible to issue shares to persons resident outside India in terms of these Regulations.

These instruments are issued by a depository abroad and listed in overseas stock exchanges like NASDAQ. The proceeds so raised have to be kept abroad till actually required in India. There are no end-use restrictions except for a ban on deployment/investment of these funds in real estate and the stock market. There is no monetary limit up to which an Indian company can raise ADRs/GDRs. However, the Indian company has to be otherwise eligible to raise foreign equity under the extant FDI policy and the foreign shareholding after issue should be in compliance with the FDI policy.

The ADR/GDR can be issued on the basis of the ratio worked out by the Indian company in consultation with the Lead Manager of the issue. The Indian company will issue its rupee-denominated shares in the name of the overseas depository and will keep in the custody of the domestic custodian in India. On the basis of the ratio worked out and the rupee shares kept with the domestic custodian, the depository will issue ADRs/GDRs abroad.

In order to bring ADR/GDR guidelines in alignment with SEBI's guidelines on domestic capital issues, the Government of India has issued the following additional guidelines on ADRs/GDRs under the Foreign Currency Convertible Bonds and Ordinary Shares (Through Depositary Receipt Mechanism) Scheme:

A. For listed companies

a) Eligibility of issuer: An Indian Company, which is not eligible to raise funds from the Indian capital market including a company which has been restrained from accessing the securities market by SEBI will not be eligible to issue (i) Foreign Currency Convertible Bonds (FCCBs) and (ii) Ordinary Shares through GDRs under the Foreign Currency Convertible Bonds and Ordinary Shares (Through Depository Receipt Mechanism) Scheme, 1993.

b) Eligibility of subscriber: Erstwhile OCBs who are not eligible to invest in India through the portfolio route and entities prohibited to buy, sell or deal in securities by SEBI will not be eligible to subscribe to (i) FCCBs and (ii) Ordinary Shares through GDRs under the Foreign Currency Convertible Bonds and Ordinary Shares (Through Depositary Receipt Mechanism) Scheme, 1993.

c) Pricing: The pricing of ADR/GDR/FCCB issues should be made at a price not less than the higher of the following two averages:

(i) The average of the weekly high and low of the closing prices of the related shares quoted on the stock exchange during the six months preceding the relevant date;

(ii) The average of the weekly high and low of the closing prices of the related shares quoted on a stock exchange during the two weeks preceding the relevant date.

The "relevant date" means the date thirty days prior to the date on which the meeting of the general body of shareholders is held, in terms of section 81 (IA) of the Companies Act, 1956, to consider the proposed issue.

d) Voting rights: Voting rights shall be as per the provisions of Companies Act, 1956 and in a manner in which restrictions on voting rights imposed on ADR/GDR issues shall be consistent with the Company Law provisions. RBI regulations regarding voting rights in the case of banking companies will continue to be applicable to all shareholders exercising voting rights.

B. For unlisted companies

Unlisted companies, which have not yet accessed the ADR/GDR/FCCB route for raising capital in the international market, would require prior or simultaneous listing in the domestic market, while seeking to issue (i) FCCBs and (ii) Ordinary Shares through GDR under the Foreign Currency Convertible Bonds and Ordinary Shares (Through Depositary Receipt Mechanism) Scheme, 1993.

It has been clarified by the Government that unlisted companies, which have already issued ADRs/GDRs/FCCBs in the international market, would now require to list in the domestic market on making profit beginning financial year 2005-06 or within three years of such issue of ADRs/GDRs/ FCCBs, whichever is earlier.

A limited two-way fungibility scheme has been put in place by the Government of India for ADRs/GDRs. Under this scheme, a stock broker in India, registered with SEBI, can purchase the shares from the market for conversion into ADRs/ GDR. Re-issuance of ADRs/GDR would be permitted to the extent of ADRs/GDRs which have been redeemed into underlying shares and sold in the domestic market.

An Indian company can also sponsor an issue of ADR/ GDR. Under this mechanism, the company offers its resident shareholders a choice to submit their shares back to the company so that on the basis of such shares, ADRs/GDRs can be issued abroad. The proceeds of the ADR/GDR issue is remitted back to India and distributed among the resident investors who had offered their rupee-denominated shares for conversion. These proceeds can be kept in Resident Foreign Currency (Domestic) accounts in India by the shareholders who have tendered such shares for conversion into ADR/GDR.

The ADR/GDR/FCCB proceeds may be utilized in the first stage acquisition of shares in the disinvestment process and also in the mandatory second stage offer to the public in view of their strategic importance.

Authorized Dealers (ADs) have been permitted to allow Indian companies to prepay the existing FCCB subject to certain conditions.

Reporting of such Issues

The Indian company issuing ADRs/GDRs shall furnish to RBI, full details of such issue in the form specified in Annexure C to Schedule 1 to Notification No. FEMA 20/2000-RB dated May 3, 2000, as amended from time to time, within 30 days from the date of closing of the issue. The company should also furnish a quarterly return in the form specified in

Annexure D, therein, to RBI within 15 days of the close of the calendar quarter.

Issue Price

Price of shares issued to persons resident outside India under Schedule-I (i.e. under the FDI Scheme), would be worked out on the basis of SEBI guidelines in case of listed shares. In other cases valuation of shares would be done by a chartered accountant in accordance with the guidelines issued by the erstwhile Controller of Capital Issues.

Permission for Retaining Share Subscription Money Received From Persons Resident outside India in a Foreign Currency Account

RBI may, permit an Indian company issuing shares to persons resident outside India under Schedule I to FEMA Notification No. 20 (i.e. under the FDI scheme), to retain the subscription amount in a foreign currency account, subject to such terms and conditions as it may stipulate.

Portfolio Investment Scheme (PIS)

FIIs registered with SEBI and NRIs are eligible to purchase the shares and convertible debentures under PIS. The FII should apply to the designated AD, who may then grant permission to FII for opening a foreign currency account and/ or a Non Resident Rupee Account. NRIs should apply to the concerned designated branch of the AD authorised by RBI to administer the PIS for permission to open an NRE/NRO account under the Scheme.

Investment by FIIs

A SEBI-registered FII/sub-account is permitted to open a foreign-currency denominated account and/or a special, non-resident, rupee account, and to transfer sums from the foreign currency account to the rupee account for making genuine investments in the securities in terms of the SEBI (FII) Regulations, 1995. The sums may be transferred from the foreign currency account to the rupee account at the prevailing market rate and the AD bank may transfer repatriable proceeds (after payment of tax) from the rupee account to the foreign currency account. The special, non-resident, rupee account may be credited with the proceeds of sale of shares/debentures, dated Government securities, Treasury Bills etc., dividend, income received by way of interest, forward contracts booked etc., by compensation received towards sale/renouncement of right offerings of shares and income earned on securities lent under SEBI's Securities Lending Scheme, 1997 after deduction of appropriate tax, if any. Such credits are allowed, subject to the condition that the AD bank should obtain confirmation from the investee company/FII concerned that tax at source, wherever necessary, has been deducted from the gross amount of dividend/interest payable/approved income to the share/ debenture/ Government securities holder at the applicable rate, in accordance with the Income Tax Act. The special, non-resident, rupee account may be debited for purchase of shares/ debentures, dated Government securities, Treasury Bills etc., and for payment of fees to applicant FIIs' local chartered accountant/tax consultant where such fees constitute an integral part of their investment process.

In the case of FIIs, the total holding of each FII/SEBI-approved sub-account shall not exceed 10% of the total paid-up capital, or 10% of the paid-up value of each series of convertible debentures issued by an Indian company, and the total holdings of all FIIs/sub-accounts of FIIs put together shall not exceed 24% of the paid-up capital or paid-up value of each series of convertible debentures. This limit of 24% can be increased to the sectoral cap/statutory limit as applicable to the Indian company concerned, by passing a resolution of its Board of Directors followed by a special resolution to that effect by its General Body. FIIs are not permitted to invest in equity issued by an ARC.

SEBI-registered FIIs are allowed to trade in all exchange-traded derivative contracts on the stock exchanges in India subject to the position limits as prescribed by SEBI from time to time. The SEBI-registered FII/sub-account may open a separate sub-account of their special, non-resident, rupee account through which all receipts and payments pertaining to trading/ investment in exchange-traded derivative contracts including initial margin and mark to market settlement, transaction charges, brokerage etc., will be made. Further transfer between the special, non-resident, rupee account and the sub-account maintained for the purpose of trading in exchange-traded derivative contracts can be freely made. However, repatriation of the rupee amount will be made only through their special, non-resident, rupee account subject to payment of relevant taxes. The AD banks have to keep proper records of the sub-account and submit them to RBI as and when required. AD banks can also offer forward cover to FIIs to the extent of total inward remittance net of liquidated investments.

SEBI-registered FIIs/sub-accounts are allowed to keep with the Trading Member/Clearing Member amount sufficient to cover the margins prescribed by the exchange/clearing house and such amounts as may be considered necessary to meet the immediate needs.

SEBI-registered FIIs have been permitted to purchase shares/convertible debentures of an Indian company through offer/private placement. This is subject to applicable ceiling as indicated in Schedule 2 to Notification No. FEMA 20/2000-RB dated May 3, 2000. An Indian company is permitted to issue such shares provided that:

(i) In the case of public offer, the price of shares to be issued is not less than the price at which shares are issued to residents, and

(ii) In the case of issue by private placement, the price is not less than the price arrived at in terms of SEBI guidelines or guidelines issued by the erstwhile Controller of Capital Issues, as applicable. Purchases can also be made of partially convertible debentures (PCDs)/ fully-convertible debentures (FCDs)/Right Renunciations/Warrants/Units of Domestic Mutual Fund Schemes.

The FII shall not engage in short selling and shall take delivery of securities purchased and give delivery of securities sold. There shall be no squaring-off of transactions during the no-delivery period of a security.

The SEBI-registered FII shall restrict allocation of its total investment between equities and debt in the Indian capital market in the ratio of 70:30. The FII may form a 100% debt fund and get such a fund registered with SEBI. Investment in debt securities by FIIs are subject to limits, if any, stipulated by SEBI in this regard.

It is clarified that an FII may invest in a particular issue of an Indian company either under Schedule 1 (i.e. FDI Scheme) or Schedule 2 (i.e. Portfolio Investment Scheme). The AD banks may ensure that the FIIs who are purchasing the shares by debit to the special rupee accounts report these details separately in the LEC (FII) returns. The company who has issued the shares to the FIIs under Schedule 1 (FDI) (for which the payment has been received directly into company's account) and under Schedule 2 (for which the payment has been received from FIIs account maintained with an AD bank in India) should report these figures separately under item 4(b) of the Foreign Currency - General Payment & Remittance return so that the details can be suitably reconciled for statistical/ monitoring purposes.

A daily statement in respect of all transactions (except derivative trade) have to be submitted by the custodian bank in a floppy disk/soft copy in the prescribed format directly to the Chief General Manager, Foreign Exchange Department, RBI, Foreign Investment Division, Central Office, Central Office Building, Mumbai 400001. to monitor the overall ceiling/ sectoral cap/statutory ceiling. When the total holdings of the FIIs reach within 2% of the applicable limit, RBI will issue a notice to all designated branches of AD banks stating that any further purchases of shares of the said company require prior approval of RBI. No purchases shall be made once the prescribed overall ceiling/sectoral cap/statutory limit is reached.

Investments by NRIs

In the case of NRIs under PIS it is to be ensured that the paid-up value of shares/convertible debentures purchased by an NRI on a repatriation and non-repatriation basis under PIS route should not exceed 5% of the paid-up capital/paid-up value of each series of debentures. The aggregate paid-up value of shares/convertible debentures purchased by all NRIs should not exceed 10% of the paid-up capital of the company/paid-up value of series of debentures of the company. The aggregate ceiling of 10% can be raised to 24%, if the General Body of the Indian company concerned passes a special resolution to that effect. The NRI investor should take delivery of the shares purchased and give delivery of shares sold. Payment for purchase of shares and/or debentures is made by inward remittance in foreign exchange through normal banking channels or out of funds held in NRE/FCNR accounts maintained in India if the shares are purchased on a repatriation basis and by inward remittance or out of funds held in NRE/FCNR/NRO account of the NRI concerned, maintained in India where shares/debentures are purchased on a non-repatriation basis. Under PIS, NRIs are not permitted to invest in the print media sector.

Shares purchased by NRIs on the stock exchange under PIS cannot be transferred by way of sale under private arrangement of gift to a person resident India or outside India without prior approval of RBI.

NRIs may invest in exchange trade derivative contracts approved by SEBI from time to time out of INR funds held in India on a non-repatriation basis subject to the limits prescribed by SEBI.

Investments by OCBs

With effect from November 29, 2001, OCBs are not

permitted to invest under the PIS in India. Further, OCBs that have already made investments under the PIS, may continue to hold such shares/convertible debentures till such time these are sold on the stock exchange.

OCBs have been de-recognized as a class of investor entity in India with effect from September 16, 2003. However, requests from such entities which are incorporated and not under the adverse notice of RBI/SEBI will be considered for undertaking fresh investments under the FDI scheme with prior approval of Government if the investment is under Government Route and with the prior approval of RBI if the investment is under Automatic Route.

The link office of the designated branch of an AD bank shall furnish to the Chief General Manager, RBI, Foreign Exchange department a report on a daily basis on the PIS transactions undertaken by it; such report can be furnished online or on a floppy disk in a format supplied by RBI.

Transfer of Shares and Convertible Debentures Non-Resident to Resident/Resident to Non-Resident General Permission

General permission has been granted to non-residents/NRIs for transfer of shares and convertible debentures of an Indian company as under:-

- A person resident outside India (Other than NRI and OCB) may transfer by way of sale or gift the shares or convertible debentures to any person resident outside India (including NRIs); this is provided that the transferee has obtained prior permission of SIA/FIPB to acquire the shares if he has a previous venture or tie-up in India through investment in shares or convertible debentures, or a technical collaboration, or a trademark agreement, or investment in the same field or allied field in which the Indian company whose shares are being transferred, is engaged. The restriction is not applicable to the transfer of shares to international financial institutions (i.e. ADB,

IFC, CDC, and DEG) and transfer of shares to Indian company engaged in the information technology sector.

- NRIs and erstwhile OCBs may transfer by way of sale or gift the shares or convertible debentures held by him or it to another NRI; this is provided that the transferee has obtained prior permission of the Central Government to acquire the shares if he has a previous venture or tie-up in India through investment in shares or convertible debentures, or a technical collaboration, or a trademark agreement, or investment in the same field or allied field in which the Indian company whose shares are being transferred, is engaged. The restriction is not applicable to the transfer of shares to international financial institutions (i.e. ADB, IFC, CDC, and DEG) and transfer of shares to an Indian company engaged in the information technology sector.
- The person resident outside India may transfer any security to a person resident in India by way of a gift.
- A person resident outside India may sell the shares and convertible debentures of an Indian company on a recognized stock exchange in India through a registered broker.
- A person resident in India may transfer shares/convertible debentures (including transfer of subscriber's shares), by way of sale, of an Indian company in sectors other than financial service sector (i.e. Banks, NBFCs and Insurance companies) to a person resident outside India, subject to the compliance with the guidelines indicated A.P. (Dir Series) Circular No.16 dated October 4, 2004.
- General permission is also available for transfer of shares/ convertible debentures, by way of sale under private arrangement by a person resident outside India to a person resident in India, subject to certain conditions, subject to the guidelines indicated in A.P. (Dir Series) Circular No.16 dated October 4, 2004.

Prior Permission of RBI in Certain Cases for Transfer of Shares/Convertible Debentures

- A person resident in India, who proposes to transfer to a person resident outside India any security, by way of gift, is required to obtain prior approval from RBI. RBI considers the following factors while processing such applications:
  - The transferee (donee) is eligible to hold such security under Schedule 1, 4 and 5 of Notification No. FEMA 20/2000-RB dated May 3, 2000, as amended from time to time.
  - The gift does not exceed 5% of the paid-up capital of the Indian company/each series of debentures/each mutual fund scheme.
  - The applicable sectoral cap/FDI limit in the Indian company is not breached.
  - The transferor (donor) and the transferee (donee) are close relatives as defined in Section 6 of the Companies Act, 1956, which is reproduced in Annex 3.
  - The value of security to be transferred together with any security transferred by the transferor, as gift, to any person residing outside India does not exceed the rupee equivalent of US$25,000 during a calendar year.
  - Such other conditions as considered necessary in public interest by RBI.
  - Applications in this regard can be submitted to the Chief General Manager, RBI, along with the documents prescribed.
- A person resident in India, who proposes to transfer to a person resident outside India any security, by way of gift, is required to obtain prior approval from RBI.
- A person resident in India who proposes to transfer any share or convertible debenture of an Indian company engaged in financial sector (i.e. Banks, NBFCs, and

Insurance companies), and which attract the provisions of SEBI (Substantial Acquisition of Shares and Takeovers) Regulations, 1997, etc., by way of sale to a person resident outside India will have to obtain prior approval of FIPB, Ministry of Finance & Company Affairs, Government of India followed by permission from RBI. The above two-stage approval is applicable even when the transfer is made on a non-repatriation basis.

Purchase of Other Securities (Schedules 4 and 5)

There is no limit on an NRI purchasing shares/convertible debentures issued by an Indian company on a non-repatriation basis whether by public issue or private placement. Amount of consideration for such purchase shall be paid by inward remittance through normal banking channels from abroad or out of funds held in the NRE/FCNR/NRO account maintained with the AD.

The NRI can also, without any limit, purchase on a non-repatriation basis dated Government securities, treasury bills, units of domestic mutual funds, and units of money market mutual funds.

As notified by Government, NRIs are not permitted to make investments in small savings schemes including PPF.

FIIs can buy dated Government securities/treasury bills, non-convertible debentures/bonds issued by Indian companies, and units of domestic mutual funds either directly from the issuer of such securities or through a registered stock broker on a recognized stock exchange in India.

A multilateral development bank which is specifically permitted by the Government of India to float rupee bonds in India may purchase dated Government securities.

NRIs resident in Nepal and Bhutan as well as citizens of Nepal and Bhutan are permitted to invest in shares and convertible debentures of Indian companies under the FDI Scheme on a repatriation basis subject to the condition that the amount of consideration for such purchase on a repatriation basis shall be paid only by way of inward remittance in free foreign exchange through normal banking channels or by debit to their NRE/FCNR (B) accounts of NRIs.

In case of investment on a non-repatriation basis, the sale proceeds shall be credited to an NRO account. The amount invested under the scheme and the capital appreciation thereon shall not be allowed to be repatriated abroad.

Foreign Investment in Tier I and Tier II Instruments Issued By Banks in India

FIIs registered with SEBI and NRIs have been permitted to subscribe to Perpetual Debt instruments (eligible for inclusion as Tier I capital) and Debt Capital instruments (eligible for inclusion as upper Tier II capital), issued by banks in India, subject to the following conditions.

a) Investment by all FIIs in Perpetual Debt instruments (Tier I) should not exceed an aggregate ceiling of 49% of each issue, and investment by an individual FII should not exceed the limit of 10% of each issue.

b) Investments by all NRIs in Perpetual Debt instruments (Tier I) should not exceed an aggregate ceiling of 24% of each issue and investments by a single NRI should not exceed 5% of the issue.

c) Investment by FIIs in Debt Capital instruments (Tier II) shall be within the limits stipulated by SEBI for FII investment in corporate debt.

d) Investment by NRIs in Debt Capital instruments (Tier II) shall be in accordance with the extant policy for investment by NRIs in other debt instruments.

The issuing banks are required to ensure compliance with the conditions stipulated above at the time of issue. They are also required to comply with the guidelines notified by the Department of Banking Operations and Development (DBOD), RBI, from time to time.

The issue-wise details of amount raised as Perpetual Debt Instruments qualifying for Tier I capital by the bank from FIIs/NRIs are required to be reported in the prescribed format within 30 days of the issue to the Chief General Manager, RBI, Foreign Exchange Department. The details of the secondary market sales/purchases by FIIs and NRIs in these instruments on the floor of the stock exchange are to be reported by the custodians and designated banks respectively, to RBI through the soft copy of the LEC Returns, on a daily basis, as prescribed in Schedule 2 and 3 of Notification No. FEMA 20/2000-RB dated May 3, 2000 as amended from time to time.

Conversion of ECB (External currency balances) Lump Sum Fee/Royalty into Equity

General permission has been granted for conversion of ECB into equity, subject to certain conditions and reporting requirements. It is also clarified that the conversion facility is available for ECBs availed either with general permission or specific permission of RBI. This would also be applicable to ECBs irrespective of whether due for payment or not, as well as secured/unsecured loans availed from non-resident collaborators. However, import payables, deemed as ECBs would not be eligible for conversion.

General permission is also available for issue of shares against lump-sum technical know-how fee, royalty, under Automatic Route or SIA/FIPB route, subject to pricing guidelines of RBI/SEBI and compliance with applicable tax laws.

Remittance of sale proceeds

Remittance of sale proceeds of an Indian security held by a person resident outside India is permissible subject to conditions stipulated in relevant Schedules to the Notification No.FEMA.20/2000-RB dated May 3, 2000, as amended from time to time. An AD can allow the remittance of sale proceeds of a security (net of applicable taxes) to the seller of shares resident outside India, provided the security has been held on a repatriation basis, the sale of security has been made in accordance with the prescribed guidelines, and NOC/tax clearance certificate has been produced.

Investments Facilities in Brief

Avenues of Investment	Nature of Instruments	Category of Investors
Public/Private Limited Companies	Shares/Convertible Debentures/Preference shares	NRIs/Non-residents/ Non-Resident Incorporated Entities/ Foreign Institutional Investors
Public Limited Companies	NCDs	NRIs, FIIs

AP (DIR Series) Circular No. 24 dated January 25, 2006.

Trading Companies	Shares/Convertible Debentures/Preference Shares	Non-residents
SSI Units	Shares/Convertible Debentures/Preference Shares	Non-residents
EOU or Unit in Free Trade Zone or in Export Processing Zone	Shares/Convertible Debentures/Preference Shares Right Share	Non-residents
Public/Private Ltd. Companies	Right Share	Existing shareholders/ Renounces
Under Scheme of amalgamation/ merger	Shares/Convertible Debentures/Preference Shares	Existing shareholders
Employees Stock Option ADR/GDR	Shares/Convertible Debentures/Preference Shares Receipts	Employees resident outside India Non-residents
Portfolio Investment	Shares/Convertible Debentures/	FIIs & NRIs

Scheme		
Investment in Derivatives	Exchange Traded Derivatives	FIIs (on repatriation basis) & NRIs (on non-repatriation basis)
Government Securities	Government dated Securities/Treasury Bills, Units of Domestic Mutual Funds, Bonds issued by PSUs and shares of Public Sector Enterprises being divested	NRIs & FIIs
Indian VCU or VCF or in a Scheme floated by VCF	SEBI-registered VCF/VC Units	SEBI-registered Foreign Venture Capital Investor

Investment in Partnership Firm/Proprietary Concern

Investment in a firm or a proprietary concern in India by a person resident outside India

An NRI or a person of Indian origin, resident outside India, may invest by way of contribution to the capital of a firm or a proprietary concern in India on a non-repatriation basis provided:

a) Amount is invested by inward remittance or out of NRE/FCNR/NRO account maintained with an AD.

b) The firm or proprietary concern is not engaged in any agricultural/plantation or real estate business (i.e. dealing in land and immovable property with a view to earning profit or earning income there from) or print media sector.

c) Amount invested shall not be eligible for repatriation outside India.

Investment in sole proprietorship concern/partnership firm with repatriation benefits.

NRIs/PIO may seek prior permission of RBI for investment in sole proprietorship concerns/partnership firms with repatriation benefits.

Investment by non-residents other than NRIs/PIO

A person resident outside India other than NRIs/PIO may make an application and seek prior approval of RBI for making investment by way of contribution to the capital of a firm or a proprietorship concern or any association of persons in India.

Investments by Venture Capital Funds

A SEBI-registered Foreign Venture Capital Investor (FVCI) with general permission from RBI under FEMA Regulations can invest in Indian Venture Capital Undertaking (IVCU), or in a Venture Capital Fund (VCF), or in a Scheme floated by such VCFs subject to the condition that the VCF should also be registered with SEBI. They can purchase equity/equity-linked instruments/debt/debt instruments, debentures of an IVCU or of a VCF through initial public offer or private placement or in units of schemes/funds set up by a VCF. RBI, on application, may permit an FVCI to open a foreign currency account or rupee account with a designated branch of an AD bank. The purchase/sale of shares, debentures, units can be at a price that is mutually acceptable to the buyer and the seller/issuer. AD banks are also authorized to offer forward cover to FVCIs to the extent of total inward remittance net of investments liquidated.

Restrictions

In terms of Regulation 4(b) and (e) of RBI Notification No. FEMA 24/2000-RB dated May 3, 2000, an NRI or PIO cannot invest in a firm or proprietorship concern engaged in any agricultural/plantation activity or real estate business or engaged in the print media.

(A) List of Activities for which Automatic Route of RBI for investment by person resident outside India is not available

1. Petroleum sector (except for private sector oil refining)/ Natural Gas/LNG Pipelines

2. Investing companies in infrastructure and services sector
3. Defense and strategic industries
4. Atomic minerals
5. Print media
6. Broadcasting
7. Postal services
8. Courier services
9. Establishment and operation of satellite
10. Development of integrated township*
11. Tea sector
12. ARCs.

* For more details, please refer to Government Manual on Investing in India, Foreign Direct Investment, Policy and Procedures. (www.dipp.nic.in)

(B) List of activities or items for which FDI is prohibited

1. Retail trading
2. Atomic energy
3. Lottery business
4. Gambling and betting
5. Housing and real estate business
6. Agriculture (excluding floriculture, horticulture, development of seeds, animal husbandry, pisciculture and cultivation of vegetables, mushrooms etc. under controlled conditions and services related to agro and allied sectors) and plantations (other than tea plantations).

Sectoral Cap on Investments by Persons Resident outside India

Sector	Investment Cap	Description of Activity / Items / Conditions
1. Private Sector Banking *	49%	Subject to guidelines issued by RBI from time to time.
2. Non-Banking Financial Companies (NBFCs)	100%	FDI/NRI investments allowed in the following 19 NBFC activities shall be as per the levels indicated below : a) Activities covered : 1. Merchant Banking 2. Under writing 3. Portfolio Management Services 4. Investment Advisory Services 5. Financial Consultancy 6. Stock-broking 7. Asset Management 8. Venture Capital 9. Custodial Services 10. Factoring 11. Credit Reference Agencies 12. Credit Rating Agencies 13. Leasing and Finance 14. Housing Finance 15. Forex-broking 16. Credit Card Business 17. Money-changing Business 18. Micro-credit 19. Rural credit. b) Minimum Capitalization norms for fund based NBFCs i) For FDI up to 51%, US$0.5 million to be brought in upfront ii) If the FDI is above 51% and up to 75%, US$5 million to be brought upfront iii) If the FDI is above 75% and up to 100%, US$50 million out of which US$7.5 million to be brought in upfront and the balance in 24 months.

		c) Minimum Capitalization norms for non-fund based activities. Minimum Capitalization norm of US$0.5 million is applicable in respect of non-fund based NBFCs with foreign investment. d) Foreign investors can set up 100% operating subsidiaries without the condition to disinvest a minimum of 25% of its equity to Indian entities, subject to bringing in US$50 million as in b) (iii) above (without any restriction on number of operating subsidiaries without bringing in additional capital). e) Joint venture operating NBFCs that have 75% or less than 75% foreign investment will also be allowed to set up subsidiaries for undertaking other NBFC activities, subject to the subsidiaries also complying with the applicable minimum capital inflow i.e, (b) (i) and (b) (ii) above. f) FDI in the NBFC sector is put on Automatic Route subject to compliance with RBI guidelines. RBI would issue appropriate guidelines in this regard.
3. Insurance	26%	FDI up to 26% in the insurance sector is allowed on the Automatic Route subject to obtaining license from Insurance Regulatory & Development Authority (IRDA).
4. Telecommunications	49%	i) In basic, cellular, value-added services, and global mobile personal communications by satellite, FDI is limited to 49% subject to licensing and security requirements and adherence by the companies (who are investing and the companies in which the investment is being made) to the license conditions for foreign

		equity cap and lock-in period for transfer and addition of equity and other license provisions. ii) For ISPs with gateways, radio paging and end-to-end bandwidth, FDI is permitted up to 74% with FDI, beyond 49% requiring Government approval. These services would be subject to licensing and security requirements. iii) No equity cap is applicable to manufacturing activities. iv) FDI up to 100% is allowed for the following activities in the telecom sector: a) ISPs not providing gateways (both for satellite and submarine cables) b) Infrastructure Providers providing dark fiber (IP Category 1) c) Electronic Mail, and d) Voice Mail. The above would be subject to the following conditions; FDI up to 100% is allowed subject to the condition that such companies would divest 26% of their equity in favor of Indian public in five years, if these companies are listed in other parts of the world. The above services would be subject to licensing and security requirements, wherever required. Proposal for FDI beyond 49% shall be considered by FIPB on case to case basis.
5.(i) Petroleum Refining (Private Sector)	100%	FDI permitted up to 100% in case of private Indian companies.
(ii) Petroleum Product	100%	Subject to the existing sectoral policy and regulatory framework

Marketing (iii) Oil Exploration in Both Medium-Sized Fields	100%	in the oil marketing sector. Subject to and under the policy of Government on private participation in: (a) exploration of oil; and (b) the discovered fields of national oil companies.
(iii) Petroleum product pipelines	100%	Subject to and under the Government policy and regulations thereof.
6. Housing and	100%	Only NRIs are allowed to invest Real Estate up to 100% in the areas listed below: i) For FD a) Development of serviced plots and construction of built-up residential premises b) Investment in real estate covering construction of residential and commercial premises including business centers and offices c) Development of townships d) City and regional level urban infrastructure facilities, including both roads and bridges e) Investment in manufacture of building materials f) Investment in participatory ventures in (a) to (e) above g) Investment in housing finance institutions, which is also open to FDI as an NBFC.
7. Coal & Lignite	100%	i) Private Indian companies setting up or operating power projects as well as coal and lignite mines for captive consumption are allowed FDI up to 100%. ii) 100% FDI is allowed for setting up coal processing plants subject to the condition

		that the company shall not do coal mining and shall not sell washed coal or sized coal from its coal processing plants in the open market and shall supply the washed or sized coal to those parties who are supplying raw coal to coal processing plants for washing or sizing. iii) FDI up to 74% is allowed for exploration or mining of coal or lignite for captive consumption. iv) In all the above cases, FDI is allowed up to 50% under the Automatic Route subject to the condition that such investment shall not exceed 49% of the equity of a PSU.
8. Venture Capital Fund (VCF) and Venture Capital Company (VCC)	100%	Offshore venture capital funds companies are allowed to invest in domestic venture capital undertaking as well as other companies through the Automatic Route, subject only to SEBI regulations and sector specific caps on FDI.
9. Trading	100%	Trading is permitted under Automatic Route with FDI up to 51% provided it is primarily export activities, and the undertaking is an export house/trading house/super trading house/star trading house. However, under the FIPB route: (i) 100% FDI is permitted in case of trading companies for the following activities: a) Exports b) Bulk imports with export/ ex-bonded warehouse sales c) Cash and carry wholesale trading

		d) Other import of goods or services provided at least 75% is for procurement and sale of the same group and not for third party use or onward transfer/distribution/sales. ii) The following kinds of trading are also permitted, subject to provisions of Exim Policy: a) Companies for providing after sales services(that is not trading per se) b) Domestic trading of products of JVs is permitted at the wholesale level for such trading companies who wish to market manufactured products on behalf of their joint ventures in which they have equity participation in India c) Trading of hi-tech items/items requiring specialized after sales service d) Trading of items for social sector e) Trading of hi-tech, medical and diagnostic items f) Trading of items sourced from the small scale sector under which, based on technology provided and laid down quality specifications, a company can market that item under its brand name g) Domestic sourcing of products for exports h) Test marketing of such items for which a company has approval for manufacture provided such a test marketing facility will be for a period of two years, and investment in setting up manufacturing facilities commences

		simultaneously with test marketing i) FDI up to 100% permitted for e-commerce activities subject to the condition that such companies would divest 26% of their equity in favor of the Indian public in five years, if these companies are listed in other parts of the world. Such companies would engage only in business-to-business (B2B) e-commerce and not in retail trading.
10. Power	100%	FDI allowed up to 100% in respect of projects relating to electricity generation, transmission and distribution, other than atomic reactor power plants. There is no limit on the project cost and quantum of foreign direct investment.
11. Drugs and Pharmaceuticals	100%	FDI permitted up to 100% for manufacture of drugs and pharmaceuticals provided the activity does not attract compulsory licensing or involve use of recombinant DNA technology and specific cell/tissue targeted formulations. FDI proposals for the manufacture of licensable drugs and pharmaceuticals and bulk drugs produced by recombinant DNA technology and specific cell/tissue targeted formulations will require prior Government approval.
12. Road and highways, Ports and harbors	100%	In projects for construction and maintenance of roads, highways, vehicular bridges, toll roads, vehicular tunnels, ports and harbors.

13. Hotel and Tourism	100%	The term 'hotels' includes restaurants, beach resorts and other tourist complexes providing accommodation and/or catering and food facilities to tourists. Tourism-related industry includes travel agencies, tour operating agencies and tourist transport operating agencies, units providing facilities for cultural, adventure and wild life experience to tourists, surface, air and water transport facilities to tourists, leisure, entertainment, amusement, sports and health units for tourists, and convention/ seminar units and organizations. For foreign technology agreements, automatic approval is granted if: i) Up to 3% of the capital cost of the project is proposed to be paid for technical and consultancy services including fees for architects, design, supervision, etc. ii) Up to 3% of the net turnover is payable for franchising and marketing/publicity support fee iii) Up to 10% of gross operating profit is payable for management fee, including incentive fee.
14. Mining	74% 100%	i) For exploration and mining of diamonds and precious stones FDI is allowed up to 74% under Automatic Route ii) For exploration and mining of gold and silver and minerals other than diamonds and precious stones, metallurgy and processing FDI is allowed up to 100 % under Automatic Route iii) Press Note 18 (1998 series)

		dated 14/12/98 would not be applicable for setting up 100% owned subsidiaries in so far as the mining sector is concerned, subject to a declaration from the applicant that he has no existing joint venture for the same area and/or the particular mineral.
15. Advertising	100%	Advertising Sector FDI up to 100% allowed on the Automatic Route.
16. Films	100%	Film Sector (Film production, exhibition and distribution including related services/products) FDI up to 100% allowed on the Automatic Route with no entry-level condition.
17. Airports	74%	Government approval required beyond 74%.
18. Mass Rapid Transport Systems	100%	FDI up to 100% is permitted on the Automatic Route in mass rapid transport system in all metros including associated real estate development.
19. Pollution Control and Management	100%	In both manufacture of pollution control equipment and consultancy for integration of pollution control systems, FDI is permitted on the Automatic Route
20. Special Economic Zones	100%	All manufacturing activities except: (i) Arms and ammunition Explosives and allied items Of defence equipment Defence aircrafts Warships (ii) Atomic substances Narcotics and Psychotropic Substances

		Hazardous Chemicals (iii) Distillation and brewing of alcoholic drinks and (iv) Cigarette/cigars and manufactured tobacco substitutes.
21. Any other Sector/Activity	100%	
22. Air Transport Services	100% for NRIs 49% for others	No direct or indirect equity participation by foreign airlines is allowed.

* Govt of India vide Press Note No.2 (2004 Series) has raised the FDI limit in Private Sector banks from 49% to 74%. RBI is yet to issue a Notification.

Terms and conditions for Transfer of Shares/Convertible Debentures, by way of Sale, from a Person Resident in India to a Person Resident Outside India, and from a Person Resident Outside India to a Person Resident in India

In order to address the concerns relating to pricing, documentation, payment/receipt, and remittance in respect of the shares/convertible debentures of an Indian company, other than a company engaged in financial service sector, transferred by way of sale, the parties involved in the transaction must comply with the guidelines detailed below:

Parties involved in the transaction are (a) seller (resident/non-resident), (b) buyer (resident/non-resident), (c) duly authorized agent/s of the seller and/or buyer, (d) AD branch and (e) Indian company, for recording the transfer of ownership in its books.

Pricing Guidelines

The pricing guidelines noted under are applicable to the

following types of transactions:

i. Transfer of shares, by way of sale under private arrangement by a person resident in India to a person resident outside India

ii. Transfer of shares, by way of sale under private arrangement by a person resident outside India to a person resident in India.

Transfer by Resident to Non-resident (i.e. to an incorporated non-resident entity other than erstwhile OCB, foreign national, NRI, FII)

Price of shares transferred by way of sale by resident to a non-resident shall not be less than:

(a) The ruling market price, in case the shares are listed on stock exchange

(b) Fair valuation of shares done by a chartered accountant as per the guidelines issued by the erstwhile Controller of Capital Issues, in case of unlisted shares. The price per share arrived at should be certified by a chartered accountant.

Transfer by Non-resident (i.e. by incorporated non-resident entity, erstwhile OCB, foreign national, NRI, FII) to Resident

Sale of shares by a non-resident to resident shall be in accordance with Regulation 10 B (2) of Notification No. FEMA 20/2000-RB dated May 3, 2000 which as below:

(a) Where the shares of an Indian company are traded on stock exchange,

  i) The sale is at the prevailing market price on stock exchange and is effected through a merchant banker registered with SEBI or through a stock broker registered with the stock exchange

  ii) If the transfer is other than that referred to in Clause (i), the price shall be arrived at by taking the average quotations (average of daily high and low) for one week preceding the date of application with 5% variation. Where, however, the shares are being sold by the foreign collaborator or the foreign promoter of the Indian company to the existing promoters in India with the objective of passing management control in favor of the resident promoters, the proposal for sale will be considered at a price which may be higher by up to a ceiling of 25% over the price arrived at as above.

(b) Where the shares of an Indian company are not listed on stock exchange or are thinly traded.

i) If the consideration payable for the transfer does not exceed Rs. 20 lakh per seller per company, at a price mutually agreed to between the seller and the buyer, based on any valuation methodology currently in vogue, on submission of a certificate from the statutory auditors of the Indian company whose shares are proposed to be transferred, regarding the valuation of the shares, and

ii) If the amount of consideration payable for the transfer exceeds Rs. 20 lakh per seller per company, at a price arrived at, at the seller's option, in any of the following manner, namely:

A) A price based on earning per share (EPS) linked to the Price Earning (P/E) multiple, or a price based on the Net Asset Value (NAV) linked to book value multiple, whichever is higher, or

B) The prevailing market price in small lots as may be laid down by RBI so that the entire shareholding is sold in not less than five trading days through screen-based trading system, or

C) Where the shares are not listed on any stock exchange, at a price which is lower of the two independent valuations of share, one by statutory auditors of the company and the other by a Chartered Accountant or by a Merchant Banker in Category 1 registered with SEBI.

Explanation:

i) A share is considered as thinly traded if the annualized trading turnover in that share, on main stock exchanges in India, during the six calendar months preceding the month in which application is made, is less than 2% (by number of shares) of the listed stock.

ii) For the purpose of arriving at NAV per share, the miscellaneous expenses carried forward, accumulated losses, total outside liabilities, re-valuation reserves, and capital reserves (except subsidy received in cash) shall be reduced from value of the total assets and the net figure so arrived at shall be divided by the number of equity shares issued and paid up. Alternatively, intangible assets shall be reduced from the equity capital and reserves (excluding re-valuation reserves) and the figure so arrived at shall be divided by the number of equity shares issued and paid up. The NAV so calculated shall be used in conjunction with the average BV multiple of Bombay Stock Exchange National Index during the calendar month immediately preceding the month in which application is made and BV multiple shall be discounted by 40%.

iii) For computing the price based on EPS, the earning per share as per the latest balance sheet of the company shall be used in conjunction with the average PE Multiple of Bombay Stock Exchange National Index for the calendar month preceding the month in which application is made and Price Earning shall be discounted by 40%.

Responsibilities /Obligations of the Parties

All the parties involved in the transaction would have the responsibility to ensure that the relevant regulations under FEMA are complied with and consequent on transfer of shares, the relevant individual limit/sectoral caps/foreign equity participation ceilings as fixed by Government are not breached. Settlement of transactions will be subject to payment of applicable taxes, if any.

Method of Payment and Remittance/Credit of Sale Proceeds

The sale consideration in respect of the shares purchased by a person resident outside India shall be remitted to India through normal banking channels. In case the buyer is an FII, payment should be made by debit to its special, non-resident, rupee account. In case the buyer is an NRI, the payment may be made by way of debit to his NRE/FCNR (B) accounts. However, if the shares are acquired on a non-repatriation basis by the NRI, the consideration shall be remitted to India through normal banking channels or paid out of funds held in NRE/ FCNR (B)/NRO accounts.

The sale proceeds of shares (net of taxes) sold by a person resident outside India may be remitted outside India. In case of an FII the sale proceeds may be credited to its special, non-resident rupee account. In case of an NRI, if the shares sold were held on a repatriation basis, the sale proceeds (net of taxes) may be credited to his NRE/FCNR (B) accounts and if the shares sold were held on a non-repatriation basis, the sale proceeds may be credited to his NRO account subject to payment of taxes.

The sale proceeds of shares (net of taxes) sold by an OCB may be remitted outside India directly if the shares were held on a repatriation basis. If the shares sold were held on a non-repatriation basis, the sale proceeds may be credited to its NRO (Current) Account subject to payment of taxes, except in the case of OCBs whose accounts have been blocked by RBI.

Documentation

Besides obtaining a declaration in the enclosed form FC-TRS (in quadruplicate), the AD branch should arrange to obtain and keep on record the following documents:

For sale of shares by a person resident in India

i. Consent Letter duly signed by the seller and buyer or their duly appointed agent indicating the details of transfer i.e. number of shares to be transferred, the name of the investee company whose shares are being transferred, and the price at which shares are being transferred. In case there is no formal Sale Agreement, letters exchanged to this effect may be kept on record.

ii. Where Consent Letter has been signed by their duly appointed agent, the Power of Attorney Document executed by the seller/buyer authorizing the agent to purchase/sell shares.

iii. The shareholding pattern of the investee company after the acquisition of shares by a person resident outside India showing equity participation of residents and non-residents category-wise (i.e. NRIs/OCBs/foreign nationals/incorporated non-resident entities/FIIs) and its percentage of paid-up capital obtained by the seller/buyer or their duly appointed agent from the company, where the sectoral cap/limits have been prescribed.

iv. Certificate indicating fair value of shares from a chartered accountant.

v. Copy of Broker's note if sale is made on stock exchange

vi. Undertaking from the buyer to the effect that he is eligible to acquire shares/convertible debentures under the FDI policy and the existing sectoral limits and pricing guidelines have been complied with.

vii. Undertaking from the FII/sub-account to the effect that the individual FII/sub-account ceiling as prescribed by SEBI has not been breached.

For sale of shares by a person resident outside India

i. Consent Letter duly signed by the seller and buyer or their duly appointed agent indicating the details of transfer i.e.

number of shares to be transferred, the name of the investee company whose shares are being transferred and the price at which shares are being transferred.

ii. Where the Consent Letter has been signed by the duly appointed agent, the Power of Attorney Document authorizing the agent to purchase/sell shares by the seller/buyer. In case there is no formal Sale Agreement, letters exchanged to this effect may be kept on record.

iii. If the sellers are NRIs/OCBs, the copies of RBI approvals evidencing the shares held by them on a repatriation/non-repatriation basis. The sale proceeds shall be credited to the NRE/NRO account, as applicable.

iv. Certificate indicating fair value of shares from a Chartered Accountant.

v. NOC/Tax Clearance Certificate from Income Tax authority/Chartered Account.

vi. Undertaking from the buyer to the effect that the pricing guidelines have been adhered to.

Reporting requirements

For the purpose the AD may designate branches to specifically handle such transactions. These branches could be staffed with adequately trained staff for this purpose to ensure that the transactions are put through smoothly. The ADs may also designate a nodal office to coordinate the work at these branches and also ensure the reporting of these transactions to RBI.

When the transfer is on private arrangement basis, on settlement of the transactions, the transferee/his duly appointed agent should approach the investee company to record the transfer in their books along with the certificate in the form FC-TRS from the AD branch that the remittances have been received by the transferor/payment has been made by the transferee. On receipt of the certificate from the AD, the company may record the transfer in its books.

The actual inflows and outflows on account of such transfer of shares shall be reported by the AD branch in the R-returns (These are returns that need to be filed with the Reserve Bank by commercial banks every 14 days) in the normal course.

In addition, the AD branch should submit two copies of the Form FC-TRS received from their constituents/customers together with the statement of inflows/outflows on account of remittances received/made in connection with transfer of shares, by way of sale, to IBD/FED/or the nodal office designated for the purpose by the bank in the enclosed proforma (which is to be prepared in MS-Excel format). The IBD/FED or the nodal office of the bank will in turn submit a consolidated monthly statement in respect of all the transactions reported by their branches together with a copy of the FC-TRS forms received from their branches to Foreign Exchange Department, RBI, Foreign Investment Division, Central Office, Mumbai in a soft copy (in MS-Excel) in by e-mail to *fdidata@rbi.org.in*

Shares purchased/sold by FIIs under private arrangement will be by debit/credit to their special, non-resident, rupee account. Therefore, the transaction should also be reported in (LEC FII) by the designated bank of the FII concerned.

Shares/convertible debentures of Indian companies purchased under PIS by NRIs, OCBs cannot be transferred, by way of sale under private arrangement.

On receipt of statements from the AD, RBI may call for such additional details or give such directions as required from the transferor/transferee or their agents, if need be.

LOANS AND OVERDRAFTS 16

NRIs are permitted to take loans in India. There are, however, some restrictions. The common restriction is that funds from any loan or overdraft should not be used for agricultural, plantation or real estate business, purchase of immovable property, shares, debentures, bonds, or for re-lending. There are two exceptions:

Loans for Agriculture

Authorized Dealers (ADs) are permitted to grant loans to resident family members of persons of Indian origin for land-based agricultural activity against the security of land held by him in India, singly or jointly with other resident members provided:

1. The loan is need-based and granted only in cases where the total land holding of the NRI does not exceed five hectares in his individual name or jointly with others.
2. The loan should be utilized only for carrying on agricultural activities on the existing land and not for acquiring additional land.
3. The loan can be repaid out of income generated from the agricultural activity or by remittances in foreign exchange sent by the NRI from abroad or by debit to the NRI's account.
4. Regulations regarding margin, rate of interest, security, etc. stipulated by RBI are complied with.

Loans for Investment

ADs are permitted to grant loans/overdrafts on a non-repatriation basis to NRIs to purchase shares or to contribute to the capital of companies engaged in the manufacturing or industrial activities, export-oriented trading, hospitals, hotels of 3 star or higher grades, shipping, development of computer software and oil exploration services subject to:

1. The concerned Indian investee company intends to issue shares to NRIs on a non-repatriation basis.
2. The period of loan does not exceed the unexposed maturity of the non-resident, external, fixed deposit pledged as security.
3. The loan should be disbursed on behalf of the NRI.
4. The loan and interest will be paid by a remittance from abroad or through the maturity proceeds of the NRI's NRE deposits. The loan can be repaid out of local rupee funds from an NRO account. The condition in this case is that the interest charged must be at commercial rates.

PERMISSIBLE LOANS

There are some that are freely permissible.

Loans Abroad against Securities Provided in India

ADs may, with the prior permission of RBI, grant loans to NRIs through their offices/branches abroad against the security of fixed deposits, shares, securities, and immovable property in India.

ADs do not require separate RBI permission to remit the sale proceeds of this security for liquidation of the outstandings, if the funds from which these assets were acquired were remitted into India and there is no bar on their repatriation.

The circular AP (Dir Series) Circular No. 69 dated February 12, 2004 has liberalized the terms of loans. ADs (banks) are permitted to grant rupee loans to NRIs as per policy laid down by the bank's Board of Directors. The quantum of the loan, rate of interest, margins, etc. on such loans may be decided by the ADs based on relevant directives issued by the Department of Banking Operations and Development in this regard. The repayment of the loan may be made by debit to NRE/FCNR/NRO accounts of the non-resident borrowers or out of inward remittances by the borrowers. ADs are not permitted to grant loans for certain activities and they must ensure that the proceeds of the rupee loans are not utilized for those purposes. The following are the activities that are not permitted with the rupee loans:

- The business of chit fund, or
- Nidhi company, or
- Agricultural or plantation activities or real estate business, or construction of farmhouses, or
- Trading in Transferable Development Rights (TDRs), or
- Investment in the capital market including margin trading and derivatives.

Loans to Employees of Indian Companies Employed In Branches outside India

Until now, loans to employees of Indian companies employed in branches outside India required the permission of RBI as such loans were treated as a loan by a resident to a non-resident. Circular AP (Dir Series) Circular No. 74 dated February 20, 2004 permits Indian companies to grant loans in foreign currency to the employees of their branches outside India for personal purposes on the same terms as they grant loans to employees in India.

Loans by Non-Residents to Residents

These can be made on a non-repatriation basis if:

1. The funds have been remitted through normal banking channels
2. The interest rate does not exceed 2% over the bank rate prevailing at the time the loan was given
3. The maturity does not exceed three years
4. The payment of interest as well as repayment of loan should be credited to an NRO/NRSR account.

NRIs are permitted to give interest-free loans without any limit to their resident relatives on a non-repatriable basis for personal purposes or for business activities of the relatives.

The NRI is, for these purposes, permitted to borrow from an AD collateralizing his assets.

Loans against Security of NRE Bank Accounts and FCNR Deposits

ADs are permitted to grant loans in India and abroad to non-residents on a repatriation basis provided the loans are fully secured by NRE fixed deposits. The loan can be repaid from funds in an NRO account but, in such cases, the commercial rate of interest must be charged.

ADs can grant loans to residents against deposits held in NRE accounts and FCNR deposits if:

1. There is no direct or indirect foreign exchange consideration
2. The term does not exceed the unexpired period of maturity of the fixed deposit accepted as security
3. The NRI should furnish an irrevocable undertaking not to withdraw the deposit before maturity
4. The loan should be for personal or business purposes
5. The loan should be granted by the bank against the NRE fixed deposit issued by the same bank and not by any other bank
6. The branch giving the loan should hold the original deposit receipt against which the loan is granted and the branch that has issued the receipt must be advised of the lien
7. RBI has stipulated in January 2007 that banks should not grant fresh loans or renew existing loans in excess of Rs. 20 lakh against NRE and FCNR deposits. In addition banks have been advised not to undertake artificial slicing of the loan amount to circumvent the ceiling.

Loans against NRNR

Loans can be granted on the security of NRNR deposits. The margin and rate of interest can be decided by the lending bank. Repayment can be by an inward remittance or by debiting the NRI's NRE, FCNR or NRO account. However, NRNR deposits have since been discontinued with effect from April

1, 2002.

Loans against NRO Accounts

Loans/overdrafts can be granted against the security of NRO fixed deposits. This is available to third-party resident individuals if:

1. The loans are to be utilized for meeting the borrower's personal requirements and/or business needs
2. The funds held in the NRO account are the borrower's and not somebody else's
3. Regulations regarding rate of interest, margin, etc. are complied with
4. Against NRO Savings Accounts, overdrafts can be permitted up to Rs. 50,000 by ADs. The overdraft must be cleared in two weeks.

Loans to Students

AP (Dir Series) Circular No. 45 dated December 8, 2003 recognized students studying abroad as non-residents. It is, however, clarified in this circular that their entitlements to loans will remain unchanged as per the provisions of Notification No. 4/2000 - RB dated May 3, 2000.

Loans against Guarantees by Non-Residents

These are permitted if:

1. No direct or indirect outflow of foreign exchange is involved by way of guarantee commission or otherwise.
2. The loan is fully secured by primary asset in the form of hypothecation or mortgage of assets or guaranteed by an international bank. The loans/overdrafts granted to a resident against an international bank guarantee should also be in conformity with the lending discipline prescribed by RBI for working capital and term loans.
3. RBI stipulations regarding margin and interest rates are complied with.

Loans to Foreign Nationals

On September 11, 1997 (ADMA Circular No. 36), the ceiling on loans to foreign nationals not permanently resident for personal purposes has been raised to Rs. 5 lakh.

Housing Loans

ADs can freely approve loans to NRIs where the NRI is the principal borrower while the resident co-borrower is a close relative or where the land is jointly owned by them. In these cases, the payment of margin money and repayment of the loan should be made by the NRI borrower. Loans can also be given to residents with the NRI as a co-obligant.

Certain institutions such as HDFC have been permitted by RBI to give loans up to Rs. 10 lakh to NRIs holding Indian passports for purchasing residential accommodation. Repayment should be made within 15 years. The loan must be fully secured by an equitable mortgage and, if necessary, by a lien on the borrower's assets in India.

Loans can also be given against the security of NRE/FCNR deposits.

If the initial deposits and installments are from money abroad, the repatriation right is protected.

If the house/apartment is rented out, the entire rental income should be adjusted towards the repayment of the loan.

General permission has been given to Indian companies to give housing loans to their NRI staff provided the remittance is from inward remittances.

IMMOVABLE PROPERTY 17

Persons resident outside India who are citizens of India may purchase immovable property in India other than agricultural land/plantation/farmhouse.

Acquisition and Transfer of Immovable Property in India.

An NRI can acquire by way of purchase any immovable property in India other than agricultural/plantation/farm house land. He may transfer any immovable property other than agricultural or plantation property or a farm house to a person resident outside India who is a citizen of India, or to a person of Indian origin resident outside India, or a person resident in India. He may transfer, agricultural land/plantation property/farm house only to Indian citizens permanently residing in India.

A person resident outside India who is a person of Indian Origin (PIO) can acquire any immovable property in India other than agricultural land/farm house/plantation property:

1. By way of purchase out of funds received by way of inward remittance through normal banking channels or by debit to his NRE/FCNR (B)/NRO account. The payment of the purchase price may not, however, be by travelers checks or foreign currency notes.
2. By way of gift from a person resident in India or a NRI or a PIO.
3. By way of inheritance from a person resident in India or a person resident outside India who had acquired such property in accordance with the provisions of the foreign exchange law in force or FEMA regulations at the time of acquisition of the property.

A PIO may transfer any immoveable property other than

agricultural land/plantation property/farmhouse in India

a) By way of sale to a person resident in India

b) By way of gift to a person resident in India or an NRI or a PIO.

A PIO may transfer agricultural land/plantation property/ farmhouse in India by way of sale or gift to person resident in India who is a citizen of India.

Interest or share in a Co-operative Housing Society or Apartment Owners Association

Though the word "immovable property" has been widely used in FEMA, no where does it define the term. Further, even the definition of "immovable property" given in the Transfer of Property Act, 1982, the General Clauses Act, the Sale of Goods Act and the Indian Registration Act, taken together, do not clarify what "immovable property" is. They only suggest what is either included or not included in "immovable property". In fact, in the above Acts, shares in the co-operative society are not so included in the definition of the term "immovable property".

However, the Supreme Court of India has made its definition clear in the case of Hanuman Vitamin Foods Pvt. Ltd. v/s State of Maharashtra (2000) by comfirning the Bombay High Court decision in Hanuman Vitamin Foods Pvt. Ltd. & Ors v/ s. State of Maharashtra & Superintendent of Stamps, Bombay (Writ Petition Number 1820 of 1986, dated 17th February, 1989). The matter of contention in this case was whether the instrument of transfer of shares in a co-operative society was an instrument for transfer of an immovable property, for purposes of levy of stamp duty thereon. The Supreme Court held, by referring to another decision in Veena Hasmukh Jain v/s. State of Maharashtra (1999) 5 SCC 725, that the agreement to sell shares in a co-operative society is, in effect, the agreement to sell immovable property.

Accordingly, any interest or share in a Co-operative Housing

Society or Apartment Owners Association (also known as Condominium abroad) is an immovable property for the purposes of these Regulations.

Refund of Purchase consideration on account of non--allotment of flats/plots/cancellation of booking/deals in respect of immovable property purchased by NRIs/PIOs in India

ADs are permitted to credit refund of application/earnest money/purchase consideration made by the housing building agencies/seller on account of non-allotment of flat/plot cancellation of bookings/deals for purchases of residential, commercial property, together with interest, if any (net of income tax payable thereon), to NRE/FCNR account, of Non--Resident Indian/Persons of Indian Origin. This is provided, that the original payment was made out of the NRE/FCNR account of the account holder or remittance from outside India through normal banking channels and the AD is satisfied about the genuineness of the transactions (refer to A.P. (DIR Series) Circular No.46 dated November 12, 2002).

Purchase/ Sale of Immovable Property by Foreign Embassies/ Diplomats/Consulate General

Foreign Embassy/Consulate as well as Diplomatic personnel in India are allowed to purchase/sell immovable property in India other than agricultural land/plantation property/farm house provided:

(i) Clearance from Government of India, Ministry of External Affairs is obtained for such purchase/sale

(ii) The consideration for acquisition of immovable property in India is paid out of funds remitted from abroad through banking channel.

Acquisition of Immovable Property for Carrying On a Permitted Activity

A person resident outside India who has a branch, office or other place of business, (excluding a liaison office) for carrying on his business activity with requisite approvals in India, may acquire an immovable property in India which is necessary for or incidental to carrying on such activity provided that all applicable laws, rules, regulations or directions for the time being in force are duly complied with. The entity/concerned person is required to file a declaration in the form IPI with RBI, within 90 days from the date of such an acquisition. The non-resident is eligible to transfer by way of mortgage the said immovable property to an AD as a security for any borrowing.

Repatriation of Sale Proceeds

In the event of sale of immovable property other than agricultural land/farm house/plantation property in India by NRI/PIO, the AD will allow repatriation of sale proceeds outside India provided;

i) The immovable property was acquired by the seller in accordance with the provisions of the foreign exchange law in force at the time of acquisition by him or the provisions of FEMA Regulations;

ii) The amount to be repatriated does not exceed (a) the amount paid for acquisition of the immovable property in foreign exchange received through normal banking channels or out of funds held in Foreign Currency Non-Resident Account or (b) the foreign currency equivalent as on the date of payment, of the amount paid where such payment was made from the funds held in NRE account for acquisition of the property.

iii) In the case of residential property, the repatriation of sale proceeds is restricted to not more than two such properties.

iv) In the case of sale of immovable property purchased out of Rupee funds, ADs may allow the facility of repatriation of funds out of balances held by NRIs/PIO in their NRO accounts up to US$1 million per financial year on production of undertaking by the remitter and a certificate from a chartered accountant in the formats prescribed by the CBDT.

Prohibition on Acquisition or Transfer of Immovable Property in India by Citizens of Certain Countries

No person being a citizen of Pakistan, Bangladesh, Sri Lanka, Afghanistan, China, Iran, Nepal, or Bhutan shall acquire or transfer immovable property in India, other than lease, not exceeding five years without prior permission of RBI.

Foreign nationals of non-Indian origin resident outside India are not permitted to acquire any immovable property in India unless such property is acquired by way of inheritance from a person who was resident in India.

Foreign nationals of non-Indian origin who have acquired immovable property in India with the specific approval of RBI cannot transfer such property without prior permission of RBI.

Loans

Loans are available for the purchase of property.

Housing Loans

Housing loans for the purchase of residential property in India and loans for repairs/renovation of residential accommodation owned by them in India are permitted to NRIs and PIOs.

Application/earnest money paid to house-building agencies refunded due to non- allotment of flat (with interest) can be credited to the NRE/FCNR account of the account holder provided the original payment was made out of the NRE/ FCNR account or if the remittance was received from abroad.

A corporate body registered or incorporated in India can grant loans to its employees who are NRIs or PIOs subject to the following:

* The loan is granted for personal purposes including purchase of housing property in India
* The loan is granted in accordance with the lender's staff welfare scheme/staff housing loan scheme and subject to other terms and conditions applicable to its staff resident in India

* The loan must be for the purpose specified, i.e. to purchase a house
* The amount should be credited to the borrower's NRO account
* It should be on a condition that repayment is by debiting the NRE/FCNR (B)/NRO/ NRNR/NRSR account or by an inward remittance or out of rental income derived from renting out the property acquired by utilization of the loan.

Indian companies in India can grant loans in foreign currency to the employees of their branches outside India for personal purposes in accordance with the lender's staff welfare scheme/ loan rules and other terms and conditions as applicable to its staff resident in India and abroad (AP (Dir Series) Circular No. 74 dated February 20, 2004)

Tax Issues

The interest paid on these loans is available both on the repayment of principal and on the interest. These are as follows:

(a) Tax rebate for principal repayment Rs. 20,000

(b) Interest up to Rs. 1,50,000 is eligible for rebate. This interest should have been paid for the acquisition of housing property.

Housing loans are available from several financial institutions and most commercial banks. The amounts vary from one institution to another. The most prominent institution is:

Housing Development Finance Corporation (HDFC)

Ramon House,

169 Backbay Reclamation,

Mumbai 400020.

On the sale of property, capital gains tax is payable. Capital gains tax is payable on the excess earned over the original cost. Certain expenses such as legal costs and brokerage are deductible from this excess capital gain. Tax is, however, not payable under Section 54 if:

(i) The residential house (original asset) is held for a period of more than three years

(ii) The seller has purchased a residential house within a period of one year before or two years after the date of transfer or sale of the original asset (the house) or has constructed a residential house (new asset) within a period of three years after the date of transfer or sale of the original asset.

(iii) Where the amount of the capital gains is not utilized for acquisition of the new asset before the due date of furnishing the return of income, it should be deposited by the assessee in an account with any specified bank or institution.

(iv) The cost of the residential house equals or exceeds the amount of capital gains.

Where the amount of capital gain is greater that the cost of the new asset, the difference between the amount of capital gain and the cost of the new asset will be chargeable as long term capital gain.

Where the new asset is sold within three years from the date of its purchase or construction, the cost of the new asset is to be reduced by the amount of capital gain exempted from tax on the original asset and the difference between the sale price of such new asset and such reduced cost will be chargeable as short-term capital gain and treated as the income of the previous year in which the new asset was sold.

Under Section 54 EC, capital gains accruing or arising on transfer of long-term capital assets will be exempted if the net consideration has been invested in specified bonds, debentures, shares of a public company, or units of a mutual fund subject to the fulfillment of all the conditions stated below:

1. The taxpayer has within a period of six months from the date of transfer or sale of the asset invested whole or any part of the net consideration in any of the bonds,

debentures, shares of a public company, or units of a mutual fund permitted/notified by the Board.

2. The cost of the specified securities is not less than the net consideration in respect of the original asset. If the cost of the specified securities is less than the net consideration, then only the proportionate capital gain will be exempted.

After availing of the exemption, the assessee has to retain the specified securities for three years from the date of their acquisition. If the specified securities are transferred or converted into money or the assessee takes a loan or advance against the security of such specified securities at any time within a period of three years from the date of their acquisition, the amount of exempted capital gain on transfer of original asset will be deemed to be a long-term capital gain:

(a) Of the previous year in which specified securities are transferred or converted (otherwise than by transfer) into money, or

(b) Of the previous year in which loan or advance is taken against security of such specified securities. It may be noted that irrespective of the quantum of loan or advance taken, the entire exempted amount of capital gain will be brought to tax.

It should also be noted that where the cost of the specified securities is also eligible for rebate of income tax under Section 88, the rebate will not be allowed if the exemption is availed under Section 54 EC.

Under Section 54 ED of the Income Tax Act, the capital gain accruing or arising on the transfer of a long-term capital asset will be exempted if the assessee has invested the capital gain in the long-term specified asset subject to the fulfillment of the conditions mentioned below:

(i) The assessee has within a period of six months after the date of transfer or sale of the original asset invested whole or any part of the central excess in long-term specified assets

(ii) The cost of the long-term specified asset is not less than the capital gain in respect of the original asset. If the cost of the long-term asset is less than the capital gain, then capital gain proportionate to part of the capital gain invested will be exempted.

After availing of the exemption, the assessee has to retain the long-term specified asset for a minimum period of one year from the date of its acquisition. If the long-term specified asset is transferred or converted (otherwise than by transfer) into money or the assessee takes a loan or advance on the security of such long-term specified asset at any time within a period of one year from the date of its acquisition, the amount of exempted capital gain or transfer of original asset will be deemed to be long-term capital gain:

(a) Of the previous year in which the long-term specified asset is transferred or converted into money, or

(b) Of the previous year in which the loan or advance is taken against security of such long-term specified asset. It may be noted that irrespective of the quantum of loan or advance taken, the entire exempted amount of capital gain will be brought to tax.

Where the cost of long-term specified asset is also eligible for rebate of income tax under Section 88, the said rebate will not be allowed if the exemption under Section 54 ED is availed. Under Section 54F, the long-term capital gain arising from the transfer of any capital asset, not being a residential house, will be exempted if the assessee has purchased or constructed a residential house subject to the fulfillment of all the conditions given below:

(i) The assessee is an individual or an HUF.

(ii) The capital gain arose from the transfer of any long-term capital asset other than a residential house.

(iii) Within a period of one year before or two years after the date of transfer or sale of the original asset, the assessee purchases a residential house or constructs a residential house within three years from the date of transfer or sale of the original asset.

(iv) Where the amount of the net consideration is not appropriated or utilized for acquisition of the new asset before the due date of furnishing the return of income, it should be deposited by the assessee in an account with any specified bank or institution.

(v) The cost of purchase or construction of the new asset is not less than the net consideration of the original asset.

(vi) On the date of transfer of the original asset, the assessee does not purchase within two years or construct within three years after that date any other residential house (other than the new asset).

If these conditions are satisfied, the capital gain arising on sale or transfer of original asset will be wholly exempted.

Where only a part of the net consideration is invested in the new residential house, then only proportionate capital gain will be exempted:

(i) After availing of the exemption, the assessee has to retain the residential house for a period of not less than three years from the date of purchase or construction, and

(ii) Should not purchase any other residential house other than the new asset for a period of two years from the date of transfer of the original asset or construct any other residential house other than the new asset for a period of three years from the date of transfer of the original asset.

If the above conditions are not satisfied, then the capital gain originally exempted shall be treated as long-term capital gain of the previous year in which such new asset is sold or another residential house other than the new asset is purchased or constructed as the case may be. The house may be let out or self-occupied.

NON-RESIDENT BANK ACCOUNTS 18

NRIs, whether they are individuals, corporates, or associations of persons can maintain bank accounts with ADs in India. The ADs in this instance are commercial banks. RBI has permitted some cooperative banks to also open accounts for NRIs. The accounts opened by NRIs can be classified under:

- Rupee accounts
- Foreign currency accounts.

RUPEE ACCOUNTS

The different types of rupee accounts a non-resident may have are:

- Non-resident (ordinary) (NRO) account
- Non-resident external (NRE) account.

There were two other accounts that non-residents could open the Non-resident Non Repatriable (NRNR) and the Non-resident Special Rupee (NRSR) account. These were discontinued with effect from April 1, 2002 and September 30, 2002, respectively.

Rupee accounts of the category mentioned below are treated as resident accounts for exchange control purposes

(i) Indian, Nepalese or Bhutanese in Nepal & Bhutan

(ii) Offices and branches situated in Nepal or Bhutan of any business carried on by a company or a corporation incorporated or established under any law in force in India, Nepal or Bhutan

(iii) Offices and branches situated in Nepal or Bhutan of any business carried on as a partnership firm or otherwise by Indians, Nepalese or Bhutanese.

It should also be noted that rupee accounts maintained in India by foreign governments and government organizations outside India are governed by regulations applicable to accounts maintained by non-resident banks. They are not subject to regulations laid down under NRO accounts.

NRO account

When a person resident in India leaves India for a country (other than Nepal or Bhutan) for taking up employment or for carrying on business or vocation outside India or for any other purpose indicating his intention to stay outside India for an uncertain period, his existing account should be designated as a Non-Resident (Ordinary) Account.

When a person resident in India leaves for Nepal or Bhutan for taking up employment or for carrying on business or vocation or for any other purposes indicating his intention to stay in Nepal or Bhutan for an uncertain period, his existing account will continue as a resident account. Such an account should not be designated as an NRO.

Non-residents may open accounts designated as NRO for receiving monies in Indian rupees. The monies in these accounts represent rupee funds/earnings in India. NRO accounts can be held by NRIs or PIOs not resident in India either singly or jointly with residents or other non-residents.

Opening of accounts by individuals/entities of Bangladesh/ Pakistan nationality/ownership requires the prior approval of RBI.

These can be savings, current, recurring, or fixed deposit accounts.

NRO accounts may be re-designated as resident rupee accounts on the return of the account holder to India for taking up employment, or for carrying on business or vocation or for any other purpose indicating his intention to stay in India for an uncertain period. Where the account holder is only on a temporary visit to India, the account should continue to be treated as non-resident during such visit.

Indians who proceed abroad for medical treatment or business visits should not have their accounts re-designated as there is no express intention of staying outside India for an uncertain, indefinite period. An NRI on a short visit does not need to have his account re-designated.

A foreign national of Indian origin, who comes to India as a tourist or otherwise can open NRO accounts for meeting local expenses. An NRO Account can be opened with funds transferred from abroad in freely convertible foreign currency in an approved manner or by funds from any local source representing bona fide transactions in rupees or by transfer from rupee accounts of non-resident banks or from an existing NRE/FCNR (B) Deposit Account or from foreign currency brought along on a visit or with travelers check. However on opening an account, with foreign exchange over US$5,000, a copy of Currency Declaration Form (CDF) is required to be presented to the bank (as proof that it came through legitimate channels). Power of attorney (POA) holders can be authorized to operate this account. As a tourist a Non-resident can place monies in a deposit account (fixed deposit). If the deposit is held for more than six months, then to repatriate the amount, permission from RBI would be required.

Credits to the account may be:

(i) Proceeds of remittances from outside India through normal banking channels received in foreign currency which is freely convertible.

(ii) Any foreign currency which is freely convertible tendered by the account-holder during his temporary visit to India. Foreign currency exceeding US$5000 or its equivalent in form of cash should be supported by CDF. Rupee funds should be supported by Encashment Certificate, if they represent funds brought from outside India.

(iii) Transfers from rupee accounts of non-resident banks.

(iv) Legitimate dues in India of the account holder. This includes current income like rent, dividend, pension, interest etc. as also sale proceeds of assets including immovable property acquired out of rupee/foreign currency funds or by way of legacy/inheritance.

Debits to the account may be:

(i) All local payments in rupees including payments for investments in India subject to compliance with the relevant regulations made by RBI.

(ii) Remittance outside India of current income like rent, dividend, pension, interest etc. in India of the account holder.

(iii) Remittance of an amount of balances in NRO account of NRI/PIO up to US$1 million, per calendar year, for all bona-fide purposes to the satisfaction of the AD.

Account holders should give an undertaking that the credits and debits in the account will be in accordance with RBI regulations.

NRIs/PIO may remit through an AD, an amount not exceeding US$1 million per calendar year for any bona-fide purpose, out of balances held in the NRO account. NRO account balances can represent the sale proceeds of assets (a) acquired in India out of rupee/foreign currency funds or (b) by way of inheritance/legacy or settlement from a person who was resident in India subject to certain conditions. It is clarified that the settlement is also a mode of inheritance from the parent, the only difference being that the property under the settlement passes to the beneficiary on the death of the owner/parent without any legal procedures/hassles and helps in avoiding delay and inconvenience in applying for probate, etc.

An NRI/PIO may remit sale proceeds of immovable property purchased by him as a resident or out of rupee funds as NRI/PIO. There is no lock-in period.

For remittance of sale proceeds of assets, both financial and immovable property acquired by way of inheritance/legacy or settlement from a person who was resident in India there is no lock-in-period. An NRI/PIO may submit documentary evidence in support of inheritance/legacy or settlement to the satisfaction of the AD.

A citizen of a foreign state not being a citizen of Pakistan, Bangladesh, Nepal or Bhutan who

(i) Has retired from an employment in India, or

(ii) Has inherited assets from a person who was resident in India, or

(iii) Is a widow resident outside India and has inherited assets of her deceased husband who was an Indian citizen resident in India.

Such citizens may remit an amount up to US$1 million, per calendar year, on production of documentary evidence in support of acquisition, inheritance or legacy of assets to the AD.

(a) The facility of remittance of sale proceeds of immovable property to a citizen of Pakistan, Bangladesh, Sri Lanka, China, Afghanistan, Iran, Nepal and Bhutan is not available.

(b) The facility of remittance of sale proceeds of other financial assets is not available to a citizen of Pakistan, Bangladesh, Nepal and Bhutan.

NRO account (current/savings) can be opened by a foreign national of non-Indian origin visiting India, with funds remitted from outside India through banking channels or by sale of foreign exchange brought by him to India. The balance in the NRO account may be converted by the AD into foreign currency for payment to the account holder at the time of his departure from India provided the account has been maintained for a period not exceeding six months and the account has not been credited with any local funds, other than interest accrued thereon.

Loans to non-resident account holders and to third parties may be granted in rupees by ADs against the security of fixed deposits subject to the following terms and conditions:

(i) The loans shall be utilized only for meeting borrower's personal requirements and/or business purpose and not for carrying on agricultural/plantation activities, or real estate business, or for re-lending.

(ii) Regulations relating to margin and rate of interest as stipulated by RBI from time to time shall be complied with.

(iii) The usual norms and considerations as applicable in the case of advances to trade/industry shall be applicable for such loans/facilities granted to third parties.

ADs/banks may permit overdraft in the account of the account holder subject to his commercial judgment and compliance with the interest rate etc. directives.

In case of a person who had availed of loan or overdraft facilities while resident in India and who subsequently becomes a person resident outside India, the AD may at their discretion and commercial judgment allow continuance of the loan/overdraft facilities. In such cases, payment of interest and repayment of loan may be made by inward remittance or out of legitimate resources in India of the person concerned.

In view of the objective of making this facility available to NRIs and the prevailing monetary conditions, RBI has directed that banks are prohibited from granting fresh loans or renewing existing loans in excess of Rs. 20 lakh against NRE and FCNR (B) deposits either to depositors or third parties. Banks have also been advised not to undertake artificial slicing of the loan amount to circumvent the ceiling.

The amount due/payable to non-resident nominee from the NRO account of a deceased account holder shall be credited to NRO account of the nominee with an AD/authorized bank in India.

The amount payable to resident nominee from the NRO account of a deceased account holder shall be credited to resident account of the nominee with a bank in India.

Persons going abroad for studies are treated as NRIs and are eligible for all facilities available to NRIs. Educational and other loans availed of by them as residents in India will continue to be available as per FEMA regulations.

ADs have been permitted to issue International Credit Cards to NRIs/PIOs, without prior approval of RBI. Such transactions may be settled by inward remittance or out of balances held in the cardholder's FCNR/NRE/NRO Accounts.

The remittances (net of applicable taxes) will be allowed to be made by ADs on production of an undertaking by the remitter and a certificate from a chartered accountant in the formats prescribed by the Central Board of Direct Taxes, Ministry of Finance, Government of India in their Circular No. 10/2002 dated October 9, 2002 [cf. A.P. (DIR Series) Circular No. 56 dated November 26, 2002].

Interest on savings accounts is at the same rate as resident accounts and can be repatriated (without prior permission from RBI) after payment of applicable taxes. The concessions allowed under Section 80L of the Income Tax Act, 1961 are also available to individuals and HUF account holders.

Non-residents are permitted an overdraft up to a limit of Rs. 50,000 (FEM (Deposit) Regulations 2000) or as stipulated by RBI (from time to time) in their savings account subject to the following terms:

- The temporary overdraft along with interest payable must be regularized within a maximum period of two weeks.
- The overdraft has to be regularized from the proceeds of fresh foreign inward remittance or out of legitimate funds from abroad or from the account holders NRE account or foreign currency deposits.

Documents required for opening NRO Accounts are:

1. Certified true copies of passport.
2. Certified true copy of Visa/Resident permit/CPR Card or any proof of residence abroad.

3. Copy of latest contracts with the company only in the case of persons employed on a ship.

If the documents are sent by mail all documents/signature/ signed photographs must be attested by the Indian Embassy/ Overseas notary/Official of the bank in which the account is to be opened.

The minimum period for a deposit is seven days.

NRE account

NRE accounts are held by non-residents with banks in India. These are opened with convertible foreign currency and the balances can be repatriated at will abroad. Withdrawals are permitted for local payments, transfer to NRE/FCNR accounts and investments permitted by RBI.

An NRE account has to be opened by the non-resident in foreign currency or by an inward remittance in foreign currency. Earlier an NRE account had to be opened when the NRI was on a visit (unless there was a branch in the country the NRI was resident in). Now thanks to the Internet, a zero-balance account can be opened from anywhere in the world. It cannot be opened by the non-resident's POA holder in India.

The account opener must, at the time of opening the account, undertake to inform the bank on relocating permanently to India. If the account is opened by the account holder from outside India, the application form should be signed/attested by an Indian embassy or notary public abroad. The account can be opened by the non-resident during his visit to India with travelers checks. The bank has the responsibility to satisfy itself that the account is in order and the account opener is indeed a non-resident. This is normally by checking the individual's passport. An NRE account cannot be opened by transfer from an NRO account unless RBI permits the transfer. The intent of these accounts is to help individual non-residents place their funds in Indian rupees to meet expenses in India or to make investments.

Only foreign remittances, travelers checks/foreign currencies or proceeds of NRE deposits or FCNR Deposits or interest on NRNR deposits should be deposited in this account. The maturity proceeds of NRNR deposits may also be credited to this account. No rupee funds should be credited to this account. These accounts are freely convertible to foreign currency and can be remitted abroad.

The accounts may be savings, current accounts, recurring deposit or term deposit accounts. A savings/current account holder is entitled to a check book. From April 29, 2003 the maturity period of NRE deposits is to be from one to three years. This applied to NRE deposits renewed after their maturity. If a bank wishes to accept deposits for a period longer than three years it may do so provided the interest is not higher than that applicable to 3-year NRE deposits.

Joint accounts are permitted provided all account holders are NRIs. A resident Indian cannot be a joint account holder. POA holders can operate the account for local payments and approved investments.

A POA or letter of authority (LOA) can be given to a resident for operational purposes. The holder can withdraw money from the account for local disbursements or for permissible investments on behalf of the NRI. They can open or renew fixed deposits by using NRE savings accounts but cannot withdraw or deposit foreign currency notes. The POA holder cannot repatriate funds held in India to accounts outside India or make gifts on behalf of the account holder to accounts held for persons resident abroad.

Interest on savings accounts should not exceed the LIBOR swap rate of US dollar of six months maturity on the last working day of the preceding quarter, and are to be fixed quarterly on the basis of LIBOR/SWAP rate of the US dollar on the last working day of the preceding quarter.

On NRE deposits of one to three years maturity the rate should not exceed the LIBOR/Swap rates of the last working day of the previous month for the US dollar of the corresponding maturity plus 50 basis points. This will be applicable in case the maturity period exceeds three years. This will apply to NRE term deposits renewed after their present maturity period. Interest should be rounded to two decimal points. As some of the banks had represented that in the absence of any directions on how to set rates based on LIBOR/ SWAP rates, banks are using different methods, sources and cut-off timings to decide the interest rates on NRE/ FCNR(B) deposits, resulting in significant variation in interest rates offered to non-resident depositor. Hence, RBI has decided that in order to ensure uniformity and transparency in interest rates on NRE/ FCNR (B) deposit, FEDAI would quote/display the LIBOR/SWAP rates which will be used by banks in arriving at the interest rates on NRI deposits. FEDAI will publish the deposit rates for five maturities in six currencies on the last working day of each month using a web page that can be accessed by all the subscribers to a Reuters screen. The first such rates were indicated by FEDAI for the last working day of February 2006.

NRE accounts can be freely converted to foreign currency non-resident (FCNR (B)) deposits. Premature closing of NRE term deposits for investment in resident foreign currency (RFC) account does not attract the provisions relating to premature withdrawal.

Transfers can be made from the NRE account of one person to the NRE account of another. Nomination facility is available in favor of any one person. The nominee can be a resident Indian or a non resident. ADs are permitted to allow remittance of funds lying in the NRE account of a deceased person to his non-resident nominee.

A loan against the balance held on an NRE account is permissible. However the loan is sanctioned subject to certain specific constraints as to its utilization. Loans against term deposits can be availed of for personal/ business purposes. RBI has permitted ADs to grant loans to NRIs for renovation/repairs/improvement to residential accommodation owned by them in India. However, loans against term deposits cannot be taken for re-lending, agriculture/plantation, or for investments in real estate. RBI has stipulated that with regard to loans to third parties against NRI deposits that the application may be forwarded through a bank branch situated in the country where the NRI deposit holder resides. RBI says that it would be preferable if such requests are routed through the bank branch at which the NRI maintains his accounts as this presupposes due diligence/compliance with Know Your Customer (KYC) norms by that branch. It is suggested that a copy of the NRI's passport be asked for along with the application for loan against NRI deposit.

These accounts have several attractions.

- The balance in these accounts including interest can be repatriated outside India at any time, without referring to RBI.
- The interest on deposits on these accounts and any other income accruing on these accounts are free of Indian Income Tax up to April 1, 2005 (this is for individuals).
- The balance held under these accounts is exempt from Wealth Tax.
- As the account holder can withdraw savings deposits at any time, banks should not mark any type of lien, direct or indirect, against these deposits. (DBOD No. Dir BC 76/13.01.09/2003-04 dated April 17, 2004).

Investments can be made on a repatriation basis on units of the Unit Trust of India/dated Government Securities/Treasury Bills/Units of any domestic mutual fund/Bonds issued by a PSU/Shares in Public Sector Enterprises being dis-invested by the Government of India/Shares and convertible debentures of Indian companies through stock exchanges under PIS/Deposits with Indian companies, NBFCs registered with RBI, HFCs and other FIs.

Investment on a non-repatriation basis can be made in units of money market mutual funds/the capital of a concern not engaged in any agricultural or plantation activity or real estate business/exchange traded derivative contracts approved by SEBI. Immovable properties, Central and state government securities, and National Saving Certificates can be purchased freely from the balances held in this account.

In regard to the operation of an NRE account there are restrictions regarding what may be credited and debited. These are:

Credits

Credits must come be through normal banking channels or deposits by an NRI when on a visit to India. Cash up to US$5,000 can be deposited. Anything higher requires proof of the NRI having signed CDF when landing in India.

A. Transactions where Form A4 does not need to be completed

i) Interest accruing on NRE/FCNR (B) accounts.

B. Transactions where Form A4 is to be completed

i. Proceeds of foreign currency travelers checks, drafts and personal checks

ii. Proceeds of foreign exchange remittances

iii. Proceeds of foreign currency, bank notes tendered by the account holder during visit to India

iv. Interest on Government securities/dividends on units of Unit Trust of India/mutual funds provided the securities/units were purchased by debit to the account holder's NRE/FCNR (B) account or out of inward remittance through normal banking channels

v. Maturity proceeds of government securities including National Plan/Savings Certificate as well as sale proceeds of such securities and units of mutual funds if these were purchased from the same account

vi. Refund of share/debenture subscription to new issues of

Indian companies if the subscription was paid from the same account

vii. Transfers from other NRE/FCNR (B) accounts of other persons

viii. Refund of application/earnest money made by house, building agencies is due to non allotment of flat/plot provided the original payments was made from an FCNR (B) /NRE account or by direct remittance

ix. Current incomes like rent, dividend, pension, interest etc provided the AD is satisfied that the credits represent current income of the non resident and the income tax has been deducted/paid, and on production of appropriate certificate from a chartered accountant (AP(Dir Series) Circular No. July 15, 2002)

x. Any other credits as may be covered by any general or special permission of RBI

xi. Current income may be credited to the NRE Account of NRIs provided the bank is satisfied that the credit represents the current income of the Non-resident account holder and income tax thereon has been deducted/ paid/ provided for, as the case may be (AP (DIR Series) Circular No. 26 dated September 28, 2002 and AP (DIR Series) Circular No. 5 dated July 15, 2002.

Debits

i. Local disbursement

ii. Transfer to NRE/FCNR (B) deposit accounts of the same account holder

iii. Transfer of NRE/FCNR (B) deposit account of other persons

iv. Remittances outside India

v. Investments in share/securities/commercial paper of Indian company or for purchase of immovable property in India provided these investments are covered by general/special permission granted by RBI

vi. Settlement of charges for the use of International Credit Cards out of funds held in Card Holder's NRE Account

vii. Any other transaction if covered under the general/special permission granted by RBI

viii. Loans up to US$250,000 to close relatives (AP (Dir Series) circular No. 24 dated September 27, 2003).

Any payments/remittances other than for the purposes of imports have to be applied in form A2. All other transactions (debt and credit) must be approved by RBI.

RBI vide its Circular No. AP (DIR Series) No.101 has permitted repatriation of sale proceeds of residential accommodation purchased by NRIs/PIOs out of funds raised by them by way of loans from a bank to the extent of such loan/s repaid by them out of foreign inward remittance received or by debit to their NRE/FCNR accounts.

On the account holder returning to India and becoming a resident the account will be re- designated as a resident rupee account or converted to an RFC account (if eligible and on the account holder seeking this option). With regard to interest income after the account holder returns to India, interest will be at the rate originally agreed upon up to maturity (for term deposits).

NRIs can take overdrafts up to Rs. 50,000. These overdrafts have to be returned within two weeks (with interest) by an inward remittance from abroad or by transfer of funds held in other NRE/FCNR accounts.

NRE accounts are held in rupees. The accounts are therefore exposed to the risk of foreign exchange fluctuations. Moreover, as the balance is in rupees, losses are incurred when the foreign currency is converted from a foreign currency into rupees and then later re-converted to dollars when the remittances or payments have to be made abroad.

Payment of interest on term deposit maturing on holiday/ Sunday/non-business working day

The bank should pay interest at the originally contracted rate on the deposit amount for a holiday/Sunday/non-working business day intervening between the date of the expiry of the specified term of the deposit and the date of payment of the proceeds of the deposit on the succeeding working day.

Interest on overdue deposits

RBI has decided (DBOD No. Dir. BC. 69/13 03.00/ 2003-04 dated February 13, 2004) that all aspects concerning renewal of overdue deposits may be decided by individual banks subject to their Board laying down a transparent policy in this regard and the customers being notified the terms and conditions of renewal including interest rates, at the time of acceptance of deposit. The policy should be non-discretionary and non-discriminatory.

It also states that the existing instructions states that banks are free to renew overdue deposits at an interest rate prevailing on the date of maturity provided the depositor approaches the bank within 14 days from the date of maturity. In case the application is made 14 days after the date of maturity the rate of interest offered should be the rate prevailing on the date of renewal of the deposit. Banks have the freedom on the interest payable for the period between the date of maturity and date of renewal. The bank is free to recover the interest so paid for the overdue interest if the deposit is withdrawn before completion of the minimum period prescribed under the scheme, after renewal.

Banks should maintain a reasonable margin on any financial accommodation allowed against the security of a term deposit and that they may determine the margin on a case to case basis.

With regard to interest payable on a term deposit standing in the name of a depositor who has died, interest should be paid at the contracted rate on the maturity of the deposit. If the claimants are residents, the deposit on maturity should be treated as a domestic rupee deposit and interest should be paid for the subsequent period at a rate applicable to the domestic deposit of a similar maturity.

If the payment of the deposit is made before the maturity date, the bank should normally pay interest for the period the deposit has been held (at the rate for the period). No penalty will be charged. If the deposit is claimed after the date of maturity (the depositor dying before the maturity date), banks are required to pay the contracted rate of interest till the date of maturity. After that date the bank will pay simple interest at the applicable rate operative on the date of maturity for the period the deposit remained in the bank beyond the maturity date. If the depositor died after the maturity date, banks will pay interest at savings deposit rate operative on the date of maturity from the date of maturity till the date of payment.

If on the request of claimants, the bank splits the amount of term deposit and issues two or more receipts individually in the names of the claimants, it should not be construed as a premature withdrawal if the amount of the deposit and the period does not undergo any change.

Regarding NRE deposits, if the claimants are residents, the deposit on maturity should be treated as domestic rupee deposit and interest paid for the subsequent period should be at a rate applicable to the domestic deposit of a similar maturity.

On rupee denominated accounts, DBOD circular No. Dir.BC. 69/13.03.00/2003-04 dated February 14, 2004 states that on deposits repayable in less than three months or where the terminal quarter is incomplete, interest should be paid proportionately for the actual number of days reckoning the year at 365 days. RBI permits banks to reckon a year to have 366 days in a leap year while calculating interest. It is also stated that banks should advise their customers how they calculate interest while accepting deposits and should display this at their branches.

Balances in the EEFC and RFC (D) accounts may be allowed to be credited to NRE/FCNR (B) Account, at the option/ request of the account holders consequent upon change in the residential status from resident to non-resident.

FOREIGN CURRENCY ACCOUNTS

The different types of Foreign Currency accounts a non-resident may have are:

- Foreign Currency (Non-resident) Deposit Accounts (FCNR (B))
- Temporary Foreign Currency Accounts.

(FCNR (B)) Accounts

NRIs, persons of Indian origin/nationality, residing outside India can open FCNR (B) accounts. FCNR (B) deposit accounts are fixed deposit accounts and are maintained in designated currencies such as the US dollar, the British pound sterling, the Euro and the Japanese yen. The deposits under the scheme mean term deposits received by the bank for a fixed period and are withdrawable only after the expiry of the said fixed period; it shall also include Reinvestment Deposits and Cash Certificates or other deposits of a similar nature.

The main reason for maintaining FCNR (B) deposit accounts is to protect the account from depreciation in the value of the rupee. These are freely remittable abroad.

An FCNR (B) deposit account has to be opened by the non-resident:

- In foreign currency or
- By an inward remittance in foreign currency or
- By funds received in rupees to the non resident bank's vostro account or
- By funds that are of a repatriable nature (per RBI regulations) or

- By tendering travelers checks while on a visit to India or
- By transfer from an existing NRE/FCNR (B) account.

Only ADs/Authorized Banks are permitted to accept deposits (A.P. (DIR Series) Circular No.89 dated April 24, 2004). However, all others may continue to hold and renew existing deposits held in their books in the name of NRIs on a repatriable or non-repatriable basis, as the case may be. As non-repatriable deposits are no longer accepted, all deposits are presently repatriable.

Non-resident accounts cannot be opened by the non-resident's POA holder in India. The account opener must, at the time of opening the account, undertake to inform the Bank on relocating permanently to India. The bank has the responsibility to satisfy itself that the account is in order and the account opener is indeed a non-resident. This is normally by checking the individual's passport and examining the visa or stay permit in the country where the person resides. Nomination facility is available for these accounts

The account can be held jointly with another non-resident of Indian origin. The account may also be held jointly with minors provided the minors are also non-residents. A joint deposit account with a person resident is not permissible. At the request of all the joint holders names may be deleted/ added. The amount or duration of the original deposit should not undergo a change in any manner and all the joint holders must be non-residents of Indian nationality or origin.

Addition/Deletion of Name of Joint Account Holders

At the request of all the joint holders names may be deleted/ added. However, the amount or duration of the original deposit should not undergo a change in any manner and all the joint holders must be Non-residents of Indian nationality or origin.

FCNR (B) deposit accounts are held by banks for maturities between one year and three years. Deposits are accepted for:

- One year and above but less than 2 years

- Two years and above but less than 3 years
- Three years only.

Recurring deposits are not accepted under the FCNR (B) Scheme.

Interest

The interest earned on these accounts is in foreign currency. The interest earned can be repatriated as it is considered current income. These funds can also be credited to NRE savings accounts. RBI will not provide any exchange rate guarantee to banks for deposits of any maturity. The maturity proceeds will be payable in the same currency. There will, thus, be no foreign exchange fluctuations risk. The main reason for opening these accounts are to protect savings from depreciation in the value of the rupee. The funds can be repatriated abroad freely.

The Board of Directors or a body approved by the Board has to approve the interest rates offered on deposits of various maturities. The rate of interest earned on these deposits would vary according to the currency. Interest is paid in the same currency in which the deposits are held.

Interest is credited either half yearly or annually (at the option of the deposit holder). Penalty for premature withdrawals is chargeable on premature termination of the deposits. If these deposits are withdrawn prematurely within the period of one year no interest is payable. The penal interest on deposits held for more than one year prematurely withdrawn is 1%. This is chargeable at the discretion of the bank.

On floating rate deposits, interest shall be paid within the ceiling of the SWAP ratio for the respective currency/maturity minus 25 basis points. For floating rate deposits, the interest reset period should be six months.

The interest on the deposits is paid on the basis of 360 days in a year. Banks should pay interest at the originally contracted rate on the deposit amount for the holiday/weekend intervening between the date of expiry and the date of payment.

The interest should be calculated and paid in the following manner:

- For deposits up to one year, at the rate applicable without any compounding effect
- For deposits more than one year, at intervals of 180 days each and there after for the remaining number of days.

The depositor will have the option to receive the interest on maturity with the compounding effect.

Interest on FCNR (B) deposits should be fixed on the basis of LIBOR/SWAP rates as prevailing on the last working day of the previous month. The ceiling will be LIBOR/SWAP rate minus 25 basis points.

As some of the banks had represented that in the absence of any directions on how to set rates based on LIBOR/SWAP rates, banks are using different methods, sources and cut-off timings to decide the interest rates on NRE/FCNR(B) deposits, resulting in significant variation in interest rates offered to non-resident depositor. Hence, RBI has decided that in order to ensure uniformity and transparency in interest rates on NRE/FCNR (B) deposit, FEDAI would quote/display the LIBOR/SWAP rates which will be used by banks in arriving at the interest rates on NRI deposits. FEDAI will publish the deposit rates for five maturities in six currencies on the last working day of each month using a web page that can be accessed by all the subscribers to a Reuters screen. The first such rates were indicated by FEDAI for the last working day of February 2006.

Members or retired members of the bank's staff, either singly or jointly or the spouse of a deceased member or a deceased retired member, can at the discretion of the bank, be allowed additional interest at a rate not exceeding 1%. This is provided the depositor/s are non-residents/of Indian nationality or origin and the depositor has given a declaration that the money is his/hers.

Payment of interest on weekends/holidays

Banks should pay interest at the originally contracted rate on the deposit amount for the holiday/weekend intervening between the date of expiry and the date of payment.

Premature Withdrawal

Premature withdrawals are permitted. Banks can, at their discretion, levy penalties for premature withdrawals. Banks can also levy penalties to recover swap costs. If the premature withdrawal takes place before completion of stipulated period and no interest is payable, banks can (at their discretion) levy penalty to cover swap costs. The components of penalty must be brought to the notice of the depositor. If this is not done, the bank will have to bear the exchange loss arising out of the premature withdrawal. Conversion of FCNR (B) to NRE deposits and vice versa before maturity will be considered a premature withdrawal and attract penal provisions.

In the case of premature withdrawal of NRE term deposit for conversion into a Resident Foreign Currency (RFC) Account, the bank should not levy any penalty for premature withdrawal. If such a deposit has not run for a minimum period of one year, the bank may, at its discretion, pay interest at a rate not exceeding the rate payable on savings deposits held in RFC accounts, provided request for such a conversion is made by NRE account holder immediately on return to India. (DBOD Dir. BC 9/13.03.00/2004-05 dated July 16, 2004)

Interest on overdue deposits

Interest payable on the renewal of an overdue contract (if the overdue period from the date of maturity to the date of renewal (both days inclusive) does not exceed 14 days) is at the discretion of the bank. The rate of interest should be the appropriate rate of interest for the period of renewal as prevailing on the date of maturity or on the date of renewal (whichever is lower). Where overdue period exceeds 14 days and if the depositor places entire amount of overdue deposit or a portion as a fresh FCNR (B) deposit, banks may fix their own rate for the overdue period on the amount placed as a fresh term deposit. The rate on the deposit renewed must be the rate prevailing at the date of maturity. Banks can recover the interest paid for the overdue period if the deposit is withdrawn before completion of the minimum stipulated period under the scheme, after renewal.

The provision applicable to NRE accounts apply to FCNR (B) deposit accounts also. Also all debits and credits permissible under NRE account scheme are also permissible under FCNR (B) deposit account. It should be noted that:

(i) RBI will not provide any exchange rate guarantee to banks for deposits of any maturity.

(ii) These accounts have to be term deposits.

(iii) FCNR (B) deposit accounts have to be opened with funds remitted from abroad in convertible foreign currency through normal banks channels or from repatriable funds or by tendering travelers checks while on a visit to India.

(iv) The remittances should normally be received in the designated currency in which the account is to be opened.

(v) The maturity proceeds will be payable in the same currency. There will, thus, be no foreign exchange fluctuations risk. The main reason for opening these accounts are to protect savings from depreciation in the value of the rupee. The funds can be repatriated abroad freely.

Loans

The funds in this account are freely remittable abroad. Foreign currency /rupee loans to deposit holders against their own deposits (not against third party) can be availed of. A loan against the deposits held in this account is also permissible subject to certain constraints as to its utilization. This includes a stipulation that the loan cannot be used for the purpose of investment in India or for re-lending or carrying on agricultural/ plantation activities or for investment in farm houses/real estate.

The documents should be executed by the deposit holders themselves and not by their POA holders. The maturity of the loans should not exceed the maturity of the deposit under any circumstances. The repayment must be effected in India by fresh remittances in foreign exchange or by adjustment of the deposit. Loans up to US$250,000 or its equivalent can be given to close relatives who are resident from an FCNR (B) account.

The rate of interest charged can be without reference to Prime lending Rate (PLR). Banks can also charge a rate less than that prescribed for advances up to Rs. 3 lakh when granted to a staff member or retired staff member/spouse or spouse of deceased staff member or retired member. When a loan is granted against a third party FCNR (B) deposit, the bank can charge interest without reference to PLR on a loan up to Rs. 2 lakh.

If it is above Rs. 2 lakh then it must be at the rate prescribed by RBI.

If the deposit against which the loan had been given is withdrawn before the stipulated period, the advance should not be treated as an advance against a term deposit and interest should be charged as prescribed by RBI. A bank is permitted to determine the margin that will be kept against the loan.

Repatriation of sale proceeds of residential accommodation purchased by NRIs/PIOs out of funds raised by them by way of loans from a bank to the extent of such loan/s repaid by them out of foreign inward remittance received or by debit to their NRE/FCNR accounts is permitted. (Circular No. A.P. (DIR Series) No. 101 dated May 5, 2003)

Interest on the death of a depositor

Interest should be paid at the contracted rate. If the deposit is being claimed before maturity, the bank must pay interest at the applicable rate prevailing on the date of placement of the deposit, without charging the penalty. If the death is before the maturity of the deposit and the claim is after the date of maturity, the bank should pay interest at the contracted rate till the date of maturity. From the date of maturity the bank should pay simple interest at the applicable rate operative on the date of maturity to the date of payment.

If the depositor dies after the date of maturity, the interest paid should be at the savings deposit rate of deposits under the Resident Foreign Currency Account Scheme till the date of payment. The bank can agree to split the deposit to two or more receipts in the name of claimants separately. This will not be considered premature withdrawal. If the claimants are residents, the proceeds should be converted into rupees at the time of payment.

NRI's return to India

Deposits held by an NRI on his return to India for permanent residence can continue till maturity at the contracted rate. For reserve requirements this will be considered as a resident deposit from the date of return of the depositor. Premature withdrawal will be subject to the penal provisions of the scheme. On maturity these should be converted to Resident Rupee Deposits or RFC (if eligible) at the account holder's option. NRI policy holders who are beneficiaries of insurance claims/maturity settled in respect of policies issued by insurance companies in India may credit the proceeds to an RFC account opened by them on becoming residents.

Penal provision on premature conversion can be waived if the balance held is placed in an RFC account. With regard to interest, it should be paid at the time of conversion of FCNR (B) to RFC even if it has not run for a minimum maturity period. The rate must not exceed the rate payable on savings bank deposits held under the RFC scheme.

For all other purposes these deposits will be treated as resident deposits from the date of return. An account holder also has an option of converting these deposits into an RFC account on maturity on satisfying certain conditions. If the deposits are withdrawn before maturity, all directions of RBI including charging of penal interest will apply.

Cardholders can settle charges for the use of International Credit Cards out of funds held in the Card Holder's FCNR (B) Account.

Balances in the EEFC and RFC (D) accounts may be allowed to be credited to NRE/FCNR (B) Account, at the option/ request of the account holders consequent upon change in the residential status from resident to non-resident. Facilitation of better hedging opportunities to holders of FCNR (B) deposits, deposit holders can book cross currency (not involving the rupee) forward contracts to convert the balances in one currency to another foreign currency in which FCNR (B) deposits are permitted to be maintained at the option of the account holder. Such contracts once cancelled cannot be re-booked.

Prohibitions

No bank should:

- Accept or renew deposits over three years.
- Discriminate in the matter of interest paid on the deposits between one deposit and another accepted on the same date and for the same maturity.

  Permission to offer varying rates is based on the size of deposits subject to conditions such as:

- Banks must determine currency wise minimum quantum on which differential rates of interest can be offered.
- The differential rate must be within overall ceiling
- The rates should not be subject to negotiation.
- No brokerage or commission should be paid on these.
- No person/agency should be employed to collect these deposits on payment of commission or fees.

Temporary Foreign Currency Accounts

Organizers of international seminars, conferences, conventions etc. are permitted to open a temporary foreign exchange account. These accounts are operated for the receipt of the delegate fee and payment towards expenses including payment to special invitees abroad. ADs can open such an account subject to the organizers obtaining the prior approval from the concerned Administrative Ministry of Government of India.

Credits to these accounts

- All inward remittances in foreign currency towards registration fees payable by overseas delegates, grant, sponsorship fees and donations, received from abroad, in connection with the conference, convention, etc.

Debits to these accounts:

- Payment to foreign/special invitees attending the conference, etc., on the specific invitation of the organizers, towards travel, hotel charges, etc., and honorarium to foreign guest speakers.
- Remittance towards refund of registration fees to foreign delegates and unutilized sponsorship/grant amount, if any.
- Bank charges, if any.
- Conversion of funds into rupees.

All other credits/debits would require the prior approval of RBI.

The Account should be closed immediately, after the conference/event is over.

Overseas Corporate Bodies (OCBs)

OCBs shall not maintain NRE Accounts, FCNR (B) accounts, and NRO Deposit accounts with ADs in India with effect from September 16, 2003. All existing NRE accounts of OCBs are to be closed and balances repatriated. NRE Deposits (recurring or fixed), FCNR (B) accounts and NRO deposits (recurring or fixed) may be permitted to continue till the original maturity. The maturity proceeds of NRE deposits and FCNR (B) accounts should be repatriated expeditiously. No new NRE/FCNR (B)/NRO accounts in the names of OCBs are to be opened nor are deposits to be renewed.

Contractors

The approving authority of the overseas contract i.e. ADs/ EXIM Bank/Working group to permit project/service exporters are permitted to open, hold and maintain foreign currency account in India. Earlier project/service exporters were required to approach RBI for permission to open such accounts in India.

19

REMITTANCE FACILITIES FOR NON-RESIDENT INDIANS/ PERSONS OF INDIAN ORIGIN/ FOREIGN NATIONALS

Remittance of assets by a foreign national of non-Indian origin

A foreign national of non-Indian origin who has retired from an employment in India, or who has inherited assets from a person resident in India, or who is a widow of an Indian citizen resident in India may remit an amount not exceeding USD one million, per calendar year, on production of documentary evidence in support of acquisition/inheritance of assets, an undertaking by the remitter, and certificate by a Chartered Accountant in the formats prescribed by the Central Board of Direct Taxes vide their Circular No.10/2002 dated October 9, 2002.

These remittance facilities are not available to a citizen of Nepal and Bhutan.

The remittance facility in respect of sale proceeds of immovable property is not available to a citizen of Pakistan, Bangladesh, Sri Lanka, China, Afghanistan, Iran, Nepal, and Bhutan.

Remittance of assets by NRI/PIO

An NRI or PIO may remit an amount up to US$1 million, per financial year, out of the balances held in his NRO account/sale proceeds of assets (inclusive of assets acquired by way of inheritance or settlement), for all bona-fide purposes, to the satisfaction of the AD, on production of an undertaking by the remitter and certificate by a chartered accountant in the formats prescribed by the Central Board of Direct Taxes vide their Circular No.10/2002 dated October 9, 2002.

An NRI/PIO may remit sale proceeds of immovable property purchased by him out of Rupee funds or as a person resident in India, provided he held such a property for a period not less than ten years. If such a property is sold after being held for less than ten years, remittances can be made, if the sale proceeds were held for the balance period in an NRO account (Savings/Term Deposit) or in any other eligible investment, provided such investment is traced to the sale proceeds of the immovable property to the satisfaction of the AD. The lock-in period of 10 years has been dispensed with in November 2006.

In respect of remittance of sale proceeds of assets acquired by way of inheritance or legacy or settlement for which there is no lock-in period, an NRI/PIO may submit documentary evidence in support of inheritance or legacy of assets, an undertaking by the remitter and certificate by a chartered accountant in the formats prescribed by the Central Board of Direct Taxes vide their Circular No.10/2002 dated October 9, 2002.

It is clarified that 'settlement' is also a mode of inheritance from the parent, the only difference being that the property under the settlement passes to the beneficiary on the death of the owner/parent without any legal procedures/hassles and helps in avoiding delay and inconvenience in applying for probate, etc.

The remittance facility in respect of sale proceeds of immovable property is not available to a citizen of Pakistan, Bangladesh, Sri Lanka, China, Afghanistan, Iran, Nepal, and Bhutan.

Repatriation of sale proceeds of residential property purchased by NRIs/PIOs out of foreign exchange

There is no lock-in period for sale of residential property purchased by an NRI/PIO out of foreign exchange. However, repatriation of sale proceeds of residential property purchased by an NRI/PIO out of foreign exchange is restricted to not more than two such properties.

ADs may permit repatriation of amounts representing the refund of application/earnest money/purchase consideration made by the house building agencies/seller on account of non-allotment of flat/plot/cancellation of bookings/deals for purchase of residential/ commercial property, together with interest, if any (net of income tax payable thereon), provided the original payment was made out of the NRE/FCNR account of the account holder, or remittance from outside India through normal banking channels and the AD is satisfied about the genuineness of the transaction. Such funds may also be credited to the NRE/FCNR account of the NRI/PIO, if they so desire.

ADs may allow repatriation of sale proceeds of residential accommodation purchased by an NRI/PIO out of funds raised by them by way of loans from the AD/housing finance institutions to the extent of such loan/s repaid by them out of foreign inward remittances received through normal banking channel or by debit to their NRE/FCNR accounts.

Remittance of current income

Remittance of current income like rent, dividend, pension, interest etc. of NRIs/PIOs who do not maintain an NRO Account is allowed freely, based on appropriate certification by a chartered accountant certifying that the amount proposed to be remitted is eligible for remittance and that applicable taxes have been paid/provided for.

NRIs/PIOs have the option to credit the current income to their NRE account, provided the AD is satisfied that the credit represents current income of the non-resident account holder and income tax thereon has been deducted/provided for.

Facilities for students

Students going abroad for studies are treated as NRIs and are eligible for all facilities available to NRIs under FEMA.

As NRIs, they will be eligible to receive remittances from India (i) up to US$100,000 from close relatives in India on self-declaration towards maintenance, which could include remittances towards their studies also and (ii) up to US$1 million out of sale proceeds of assets/balances in their account maintained with an AD in India.

All other facilities available to NRIs under FEMA are equally applicable to students.

Educational and other loans availed by them as residents in India will continue to be available as per FEMA regulations.

Income-tax clearance

ADs can make remittances on production of an undertaking by the remitter and a certificate from a Chartered Accountant in the formats prescribed by the Central Board of Direct Taxes, Ministry of Finance, Government of India in their Circular No.10/2002 dated October 9, 2002. [cf. AP (DIR Series) Circular No.56 dated November 26, 2002].

International Credit Cards

ADs are permitted to issue International Credit Cards to NRIs/PIOs, without prior approval of RBI. Such transactions may be settled by inward remittance or out of balances held in the cardholder's FCNR/NRE/NRO accounts.

BAGGAGE RULES 20

Whenever one travels abroad, there is a compulsion to purchase articles. These could be for personal/professional use, or to give as gifts. All governments recognize this compulsion and permit incoming travelers to bring in a certain amount. Unlimited imports will, as one appreciates, result in a tremendous loss of customs duty. The amounts permitted and the rules regarding these are encapsulated in the Baggage Rules, 1998. These rules differentiate between different types of travelers i.e. residents, tourists and individuals transferring their residence.

However, prior to discussing the amounts permitted for each category, it is important to be clear about certain definitions and usages.

Baggage

Baggage means 'belongings with which one travels'. The Customs Act 1962 states that baggage includes unaccompanied baggage but does not include motor cars. The Baggage Rules, however, indicate that only such articles as having been in the use of the traveler and which have been bought and paid for before his departure are considered baggage. Baggage includes gifts and souvenirs. The term also includes all items brought in by a passenger and would, therefore, even include gold bangles worn by a passenger. It should be noted that goods brought through a friend or some other person who is merely acting as a carrier is not baggage. Items brought into the country in commercial quantities will not be treated as bona fide baggage and would require an import permit.

The Customs Act 1962 (Section 77) requires the owner of

any baggage to clear it and make a full declaration of its contents to the proper officer. The onus is on the passenger. Any items that do not correspond with the declaration, made in respect of valuation, description or any other matter, can be confiscated by the customs authorities. Additionally, a person carrying foreign goods to India without a valid license and without declaring them is liable to be penalized even if the goods did not actually belong to him. Mis-declaration or no declaration entails penal action. Items brought in excess of the quantities/ value permitted, attracts duty.

If baggage constitutes an article, on which duty is levied, or the import of which is prohibited and the passenger has made a proper declaration, the passenger can ask the customs officer to detain the article and to have it returned to him on him leaving India. Similarly, if he wishes to bring into the country an item without the payment of duty, he can ask the customs officer to describe the article in his passport with the understanding that on his leaving India, he would produce the article to the customs officer.

The current rate of customs duty on baggage is 40%.

These rules have been effective from June 30, 2006.

Definitions

In these rules, unless the context otherwise requires,-

(i) "appendix" means an Appendix to these rules

(ii) "resident" means a person holding a valid passport issued under the Passports Act, 1967 (15 of 1967) and normally residing in India

(iii) "tourist" means a person not normally resident in India, who enters India for a stay of not more than six months in the course of any twelve months period for legitimate non-immigrant purposes, such as touring, recreation, sports, health, family reasons, study, religious pilgrimage or business

(iv) "family" includes all persons who are residing in the same house and form part of the same domestic establishment

(v) "professional equipment" means such portable equipments, instruments, apparatus and appliances as are required in his profession, by a carpenter, a plumber, a welder, a mason, and the like and shall not include items of common use such as cameras, cassette recorders, dictaphones, personal computers, typewriters, and other similar articles.

Passengers returning from countries other than Nepal, Bhutan, Myanmar, or China

An Indian resident or a foreigner residing in India, returning from any country other than Nepal, Bhutan, Myanmar, or China, shall be allowed clearance free of duty articles in his bona fide baggage to the extent mentioned in column (2) of Appendix A.

Provided that such Indian resident or such foreigner coming by land route as specified in Annexure IV, shall be allowed clearance free of duty articles in his bonafide baggage to the extent mentioned in column (2) of Appendix 'B'."

Passengers returning from Nepal, Bhutan, Myanmar, or China

An Indian resident or a foreigner residing in India, returning from Nepal, Bhutan, Myanmar or China, other than by land route, shall be allowed clearance free of duty articles in his bona fide baggage to the extent mentioned in column (2) of Appendix B.

Professionals returning to India

An Indian passenger who was engaged in his profession abroad shall on his return to India be allowed clearance free of duty, in addition to what he is allowed under rule 3 or, as the case may be, under rule 4, articles in his bona fide baggage to the extent mentioned in column (2) of Appendix C.

Jewelry

A passenger returning to India shall be allowed clearance free of duty jewelry in his bona fide baggage to the extent mentioned in column (2) of Appendix D.

Tourists

A tourist arriving in India shall be allowed clearance free of duty articles in his bona fide baggage to the extent mentioned in column (2) of Appendix E.

Transfer of Residence

(1) A person who is transferring his residence to India shall be allowed clearance free of duty, in addition to what he is allowed under rule 3 or, as the case may be, under rule 4, articles in his bona fide baggage to the extent mentioned in column (1) of Appendix F, subject to the conditions, if any, mentioned in the corresponding entry in column (2) of the said Appendix.

(2) The conditions may be relaxed to the extent mentioned in column (3) of the said Appendix.

Provisions regarding unaccompanied baggage

(1) Provisions of these Rules are also extended to unaccompanied baggage except where they have been specifically excluded.

(2) The unaccompanied baggage had been in the possession abroad of the passenger and is dispatched within one month of his arrival in India or within such further period as the Assistant Commissioner of Customs or Deputy Commissioner of Customs may allow.

(3) The unaccompanied baggage may land in India up to 2 months before the arrival of the passenger or within such period, not exceeding one year, as the Assistant Commissioner of Customs or Deputy Commissioner of Customs may allow, for reasons to be recorded, if he is satisfied that the passenger was prevented from arriving in India within the period of two months due to circumstances beyond his control such as sudden illness of the passenger or a member of his family, or natural calamities or disturbed conditions or disruption of the transport or travel arrangements in the country or countries concerned or

any other reasons, which necessitated a change in the travel schedule of the passenger.

Application of these rules to members of the crew

The provisions of these Rules shall apply in respect of members of the crew engaged in a foreign going vessel for importation of their baggage at the time of final pay off on termination of their engagement.

Provided that except as specified in this sub-rule, a crew member of a vessel shall be allowed to bring items like chocolates, cheese, cosmetics and other petty gift items for their personal or family use which shall not exceed the value of Rs. 600.

(2) Notwithstanding anything contained in these rules a crew member of an aircraft shall be allowed to bring items gifts like chocolates, cheese, cosmetics and other petty gift items at the time of the returning of the aircraft from foreign journey for their personal or family use which shall not exceed the value of Rs. 600.

Appendix A

(See rule 3)

(1)	Articles allowed free of duty (2)
(a) All passengers of and above 10 years of age and returning after stay abroad of more than three days.	(i) Used personal effects, excluding jewelry, required for satisfying daily necessities of life. (ii) Articles other than those mentioned in Annexure I up to a value of Rs. 25,000 if these are carried on the person or in the accompanied baggage of the passenger.

(b) All passengers of and above 10 years of age and returning after stay abroad of three days or less.	(i) Used personal effects, excluding jewelry, required for satisfying daily necessities of life. (ii) Articles other than those mentioned in Annexure I up to a value of Rs. 12,000 if these are carried on the person or in the accompanied baggage of the passenger.
(c) All passengers up to 10 years of age and returning after stay abroad of more than three days.	(i) Used personal effects, excluding jewelry, required for satisfying daily necessities of life. (ii) Articles other than those mentioned in Annexure I up to a value of Rs. 6,000 if these are carried on the person or in the accompanied baggage of the passenger.
(d) All passengers up to 10 years of age and returning after stay abroad of three days or less.	(i) Used personal effects, excluding jewelry, required for satisfying daily necessities of life. (ii) Articles other than those mentioned in Annexure I up to a value of Rs. 3,000 if these are carried on the person or in the accompanied baggage of the passenger.

Explanation - The free allowance under this rule shall not be allowed to be pooled with the free allowance of any other passenger.

Appendix B

(See rule 3)

(1)	(2)
(i) Passengers of and above 10 years of age and returning after stay abroad of more than three days.	(i) Used personal effects, excluding jewelry, required for satisfying daily necessities of life. (ii) Articles other than those mentioned in Annexure I up to a value of Rs. 6,000 if these are carried on the person or in the accompanied baggage of the passenger.
(ii) Passengers up to 10 years of age and returning after stay abroad of more than three days.	(i) Used personal effects, excluding jewelry, required for satisfying daily necessities of life. (ii) Articles other than those mentioned in Annexure I up to a value of Rs. 1500 if these are carried on the person or in the accompanied baggage of the passenger.

Explanation - The free allowance under this rule shall not be allowed to be pooled with the free allowance of any other passenger.

Appendix C (See rule 5) (1)	Articles allowed free of duty (2)
(a) Indian passenger returning after at least 3 months.	(i) Used household articles up to an aggregate value of Rs. 12,000 (ii) Professional equipment up to a value of Rs. 20,000.
(b) Indian passenger returning after at least 6 months.	(i) Used household articles up to an aggregate value of Rs.12,000 (ii) Professional equipment up to a value of Rs. 40,000.
(c) Indian passenger returning after a stay of minimum 365 days during the preceding two years on termination of his work, and who has not availed this concession in the preceding three years.	(i) Used household articles and personal effects, (which have been in the possession and use abroad of the passenger or his family for at least six months), and which are not mentioned in Annex I, Annexure II or Annexure III up to an aggregate value of Rs. 75,000.

(Item (c), in column(2), in entry (i), for the figures 30,000, the figures 75,000 has been substituted vide Notification No. 11/2002 - Customs (N.T.) dated March 1st, 2002)

Appendix D
(See rule 6)

(1)	(2) Jewelry
(Indian passenger who has been residing abroad for over one year.	(i) Jewelry up to an aggregate value of Rs.10,000 by a gentleman passenger, or (ii) Up to aggregate value of Rs. 20,000 by a lady passenger.

Appendix E
(See rule 7)

(1)	Articles allowed free of duty (2)
(a) Tourists of Indian origin coming to India other than tourists of Indian origin coming by land routes as specified in Annexure IV	(i) used personal effects and travel souvenirs, if: (a) these goods are for personal use of the tourist (b) these goods, other than those consumed during the stay in India, are re-exported when the tourist leaves India for a foreign destination. (ii) articles as allowed to be cleared under rule 3 or rule 4.
(b) Tourists of foreign origin other than those	(i) used personal effects and travel souvenirs, if:

of Nepalese origin coming from Nepal or of Bhutanese origin coming Bhutan or of Pakistani origin coming from Pakistan.	(a) these goods are for personal use of the tourist (b)these goods, other than those consumed during the stay in India, are re-exported when the tourist leaves India for a foreign destination. (ii) articles up to a value of Rs. 8000 for making gifts.
(c) Tourists of Nepalese origin coming from Nepal or of Bhutanese origin coming from Bhutan.	No free allowance.
(d) Tourists (i) of Pakistani origin coming from Pakistan other than by land routes;	(i) used personal effects and travel souvenirs, if: (a) these goods are for personal use of the tourist
(ii) of Pakistani origin or foreign tourists coming by land routes as specified in Annexure IV; (iii) of Indian origin coming by land routes as specified in Annexure IV.	(b)these goods, other than those consumed during the stay in India, are re exported when the tourist leaves India for a foreign destination. (ii) articles up to a value of Rs. 6000 for making gifts.

Appendix F
(See rule 8)

Articles allowed free of duty	Conditions	Relaxation that may be considered
(a) Used personal and household articles, other than those listed at Annexure. I or Annexure II, but including the article listed at Annexure III and jewelry up to Rs. 10,000 by a gentleman passenger or Rs. 20,000 by a lady passenger.	(1) Minimum stay of two years abroad, immediately preceding the date of his arrival on TR, (2) total stay in India on short visit during the Two preceding years should not exceed Six months, and (3) passenger has not availed this concession in the preceding three years.	(a) For condition (1) Shortfall of up to two months in stay abroad can be condoned by Assistant Commissioner of Customs or Deputy Commissioner of Customs if the early return is on account of : (i) terminal leave or vacation being availed of by the passenger; or (ii) any other special circumstances. (b) For condition (2) Commissioner of Customs may condone short visits in excess of 6 months in deserving cases. (c) For condition (3) **No relaxation**
(b) Jewelry taken out earlier by the passenger or by a member of his family from India.	Satisfaction of the Assistant Commissioner of Customs regarding the jewelry having been taken out earlier from India.	

Annexure I

1. Firearms.
2. Cartridges of firearms exceeding 50 in number.
3. Cigarettes exceeding 200 or cigars exceeding 50 or tobacco exceeding 250 gms.
4. Alcoholic liquor or wines in excess of two liters.
5. Gold or silver, in any form, other than ornaments.

Annexure II

1. Colour Television or Monochrome Television.
2. Digital Video Disc Player.
3. Video Home Theatre System.
4. Dish Washer.
5. Music System.
6. Air-Conditioner.
7. Domestic refrigerators of capacity above 300 liters or its equivalent.
8. Deep Freezer.
9. Microwave Oven.
10. Video camera or the combination of any such video camera with one or more of the following goods, namely:
    a) Television Receiver
    b) Sound recording or reproducing apparatus
    c) Video reproducing apparatus.
11. Word Processing Machine.
12. Fax Machine.
13. Portable Photocopying Machine.
14. Vessel.
15. Aircraft.
16. Cinematographic films of 35 mm and above.
17. Gold or Silver, in any form, other than ornaments.

Annexure III

1. Video Cassette Recorder or Video Cassette Player or Video Television Receiver or Video Cassette Disk Player.
2. Washing Machine.
3. Electrical or Liquefied Petroleum Gas Cooking Range.

4. Personal Computer (Desktop Computer).
5. Laptop Computer (Notebook Computer).
6. Domestic Refrigerators of capacity up to 300 liters or its equivalent.

Annexure IV

Amritsar:
(1) Amritsar Railway Station
(2) Attari Road
(3) Attari Railway Station
(4) Khalra

Baroda:
(5) Assara Naka
(6) Khavda Naka
(7) Lakhpat
(8) Santalpur Naka
(9) Suigam Naka

Delhi:
(10) Delhi Railway Station

Ferozpur District:
(11) Hussainiwala

Jodhpur Division:
(12) Barmer Railway Station
(13) Munabao Railway Station

Baramullah District:
(14) Adoosa

Poonch District:
(15) Chakan-da-bagh

IMPORT OF GOLD AND SILVER 21

Gold

Passengers (including minor children) holding Indian passports or of Indian origin can bring gold up to 10 kilograms per passenger after a stay of six months abroad. Short visits up to 30 days duration are ignored. Gold includes primary gold ornaments other than those studded with stones or pearls.

The passenger can bring the gold or silver himself at the time of arrival or import the same within 15 days of his arrival in India.

The passenger can also obtain the permitted quantity of gold/silver from customs bonded warehouse of the State Bank of India (SBI) and the Mineral and Metal Trading Corporation (MMTC). The passenger is required to file a declaration on the prescribed form before the customs officer at the time of arrival in India stating his intention to obtain the gold/silver from the customs bonded warehouse and pay the duty before clearance. Delivery will be at the city in which the passenger disembarked. The passenger has the option to pay for the gold/silver in foreign exchange either abroad or in India. In cases where the payment has been made abroad and the passenger was found ineligible to import the gold, he will obtain a refund. The eligibility of the passengers is decided by the customs authorities at the time of customs clearance.

Import of personal jewelry, which is worn by the passenger and is part of personal baggage, may be made without a license provided that the value does not exceed the limit specified/ import free of customs duty.

It should be remembered that a passenger who has been residing abroad for over a year and is returning to India may be allowed to import free of duty jewelry (both gold and silver) in his use up to an aggregate value of Rs. 10,000 in the case of a male passenger and Rs. 20,000 in the case of a female passenger. Jewelry, which is additional to the jewelry otherwise allowed without payment of duty (under the Baggage Rules), is only liable for payment of duty for import of gold. Gold, not declared, is liable for confiscation.

Only a moderate duty of Rs. 250* per 10 grams of gold is payable in convertible foreign exchange. Nationals of Pakistan and Bangladesh shall not be deemed to be of Indian origin. (*The Finance Act 2003 reduced the import duty on gold to Rs. 100 per 10 grams). However, if the imported gold is in the form of gold bars (other than tola bars) bearing the manufacturer's or refiner's engraved serial numbers and the weight expressed in metric units, and on gold coins, the duty will be Rs. 100 per 10 grams.

In order to pay duty by convertible foreign currency, the eligible passenger must bring the foreign currency along with him when he returns to India. If the foreign currency is to be brought into India, then there must be an endorsement to that effect in the passport of the passenger. If there is no endorsement and duty is paid in convertible foreign currency, the said passenger is duty bound to explain the source of the currency.

Silver

With regard to silver, the import is allowed in any form including ornaments (excluding stones or pearls) by an eligible passenger at a concessional duty of Rs. 500 per kilogram subject to the following:

(a) The duty at the rate of Rs. 500 per kilogram is paid in convertible foreign currency;

(b) The quantity of silver does not exceed 100 kilograms per passenger;

(c) The silver either is carried by the passenger at the time of his arrival in India or is imported by him within 15 days of his arrival in India.

The exemption will also apply to silver that is taken delivery of by an eligible passenger from a customs bonded warehouse of SBI or MMTC, provided that the passenger files a declaration before the proper officer of customs at the time of his arrival in India declaring his intention to take delivery of the silver from a customs bonded warehouse and pays the duty to be levied thereon before his clearance from customs.

Passengers who have been residing abroad for over a year and are returning to India may be allowed to import free of duty silver/gold jewelry up to an aggregate value of Rs. 10,000 in the case of a male passenger and Rs. 20,000 in the case of a female passenger.

There are no restrictions on the import of foreign coins made of gold or any other metal. The same holds good in respect of commemorative coins also.

Gold/silver brought into India by persons of Indian nationality/origin while coming into India may sell it to residents against payment in rupees.

IMPORT OF CARS AND VEHICLES 22

Import of cars and vehicles without a license by Indian nationals and persons of Indian origin is permitted subject to certain conditions.

Conditions for Import

1. A car of an engine size not exceeding four cylinders with power not more than 1600cc may be imported. It does not matter whether the car is new or old. However, if a car has been in the use of the importer for more than a year, he can import the car on his return to India even if its engine size exceeds four cylinders and is more than 1600cc.
2. The importer should, at the time of import, declare that he is returning to India for permanent residence.
3. The importer has stayed abroad continuously for a minimum of two years prior to his returning to India.
4. The payment for the car is made abroad in foreign currency.
5. The customs duty at the time of import is made in foreign exchange.
6. The car should be imported into India within six months of the arrival of the importer in India for permanent residence.
7. Should an importer transfer his residence out of India, he may import another car only after a minimum of five years from the date of import of the earlier vehicle.
8. All such imports carry a 'no sale' condition of two years.

At the time of Import

At the time of importing the car, the importer has to produce his passport, the registration books of the vehicle and the insurance policy for the vehicle.

Valuation

The customs duty which has to be paid on foreign currency is based on the vehicle's valuation. There is a strict formula followed to determine the valuation:

(a) The ex-factory list price in the country of manufacture on the date on which the bill of entry is presented, less trade discount and depreciation. To this, freight and insurance charges from the country of manufacture to India, and landing charges are added.

(b) Depreciation is calculated from the date of registration of the car in the owner's name and the date of the actual shipment of the vehicle or the date of departure of the owner from the foreign country (whichever is earlier). The rate of depreciation is based on the ex-factory price and is at the following rates.

1st year	4% per quarter or part thereof
2nd year	3% per quarter or part thereof
3rd year	2 S % per quarter or part thereof
4th year & thereafter	2% per quarter or part thereof

The maximum depreciation permitted is 70%.

Import Duty Rates

Import duty rates vary and will depend on the rate at the time the vehicle is imported.

Sale of Vehicle

Vehicles imported into India can be freely sold after the expiry of the 'no sale' period of two years. This facility is only available to Indians or persons of Indian origin who have returned to India for permanent residence.

23

EXPORT OF JEWELRY, INDIAN CURRENCY, FOREIGN EXCHANGE, SECURITIES, ETC

Export of Jewelry

The export of personal jewelry out of India by travelers is regulated under the Baggage Rules framed by the Ministry of Commerce under the Export-Import Policy.

The Export-Import Policy does not lay any restrictions on the export of any goods (including gold jewelry) as baggage, provided that it is bona fide baggage of the traveler.

Export of Indian Currency

The export of Indian currency notes and coins is prohibited without the special permission of RBI. There are general permissions, however, which are:

(i) To Nepal - Indian currency notes of denominations up to Rs. 100 and Indian coins by any person without limit.

(ii) To countries other than Nepal - Indian currency notes and coins not exceeding Rs. 5000 per person by any resident Indian proceeding abroad on a temporary visit.

(iii) Commemorate coins of up to two coins each of Rs. 50 and Rs. 10 denomination can be sent out.

Indian currency exported or attempted to be exported except within the terms of the general or special permission granted by RBI is liable to be confiscated and the offenders may be liable for punishment.

Export of Foreign Exchange

The export of foreign exchange in any form, including currency notes or bank notes other than foreign exchange obtained from an AD/authorized money changer by the person exporting it, is prohibited unless it is covered by a general or special permission of RBI.

RBI has granted general permission to persons resident in India to take out of India foreign currency or currencies equivalent to US$10,000 every year for personal purposes.

Persons in India but not resident in India will be permitted by customs to take out of India their unspent foreign currency provided that they had declared the import to customs at the time of arrival.

ADs may sell foreign currency notes and coins to travelers traveling abroad only in conformity with the provisions of the Exchange Control Manual (Chapter 3). Foreign currency notes/coins thus acquired will be endorsed by the AD on the traveler's passport.

Export of Checks by ADs and Others

ADs are permitted to send out of India foreign currency in the form of currency notes, coins, checks, drafts or bills of exchange acquired by them in the normal course of their business and within the terms of their authorization.

Foreign citizens resident in India but not permanently resident in India and resident Indians maintaining foreign currency accounts abroad are permitted to take or send out of India checks drawn on their foreign currency accounts.

Export of Securities

RBI's permission is required for the export of securities out of India. Those in India holding foreign securities who wishes to send them out of India for sale or transfer should apply to RBI for an export permit through an AD. Permission for export will be granted provided that the AD gives an undertaking in the case of sale that the foreign currency proceeds of the securities sold will be repatriated to India, and in the case of transfer that the securities after transfer will be received back in India within a reasonable period. These restrictions do not apply to the export of securities outside by a person who has returned to India after a continuous stay of not less than one year abroad. Additionally, RBI has granted general permission to export certificates covering units purchased by non-resident investors from out of foreign exchange remittances in India or from their non-resident accounts in India.

IMPORT AND EXPORT OF GIFTS 24

Import of Gifts

Gifts can be made to friends and relatives in India without a customs clearance permit if:

(i) The gift is made for the donee's personal use;

(ii) The gift is made by post or otherwise.

(iii) The CIF (cost insurance freight) value of the gift parcel does not exceed Rs. 2,000 and does not contain items which are not permitted to be imported, canalized items, alcoholic beverages, fire arms and ammunition, and consumer electronic items (except hearing aids and life-saving equipment).

(iv) The gift is of consumer goods to charitable, religious or educational institutions and such persons/bodies, which may be approved by the Central Government. The value of gifts brought by tourists of foreign and Indian origin that are exempted from duty is based on that determined under the Baggage Rules.

If gifts that are not freely importable are to be brought in, a customs clearance permit is required.

Exports of Gifts

Items/goods of up to Rs. 1 lakh in a licensing year may be exported as a gift. Items restricted for export cannot be exported without a license. This was increased to Rs. 5 lakh from February 20, 2004 (AP (Dir Series) Circular No. 73 dated February 20, 2004).

Transfer of security by way of gift

A person resident in India who proposes to transfer, by way of gift, to a person resident outside India any security including shares/convertible debentures is required to obtain prior approval of RBI. The application has to be submitted along with certain information/documents, a list of which is detailed below to the Chief General Manager, Reserve Bank of India, Foreign Exchange Department, Foreign Investment Division, Central Office, 11th floor, Fort, Mumbai 400 001.

RBI would, henceforth, consider the following factors while considering such applications:

a. The transferee (donee) is eligible to hold such security.
b. The gift does not exceed 5% of the paid-up capital of the Indian company/each series of debentures/each mutual fund scheme.
c. The applicable sectoral cap/foreign direct investment (FDI) limit in the Indian company is not breached.
d. The transferor (donor) and the transferee (donee) are close relatives as defined in section 6 of the Companies Act, 1956.
e. The value of security to be transferred together with any security transferred by the transferor, as gift, to any person residing outside India does not exceed the rupee equivalent of US$25,000 during a calendar year.
f. Such other conditions as considered necessary in public interest by RBI.

Information/Documents to be submitted along with the application to RBI by a person resident in India who proposes to transfer to a person resident outside India any security including shares/convertible debentures, by way of gift

1. Name and address of the transferor (donor) and the transferee (donee).
2. Relationship between the transferor and the transferee.
3. Reasons for making the gift.
4. In case of dated Government securities and treasury bills and bonds, a certificate issued by a chartered accountant on the market value of such security.

5. In case of units of domestic mutual funds and units of Money Market Mutual Funds, a certificate from the issuer on the Net Asset Value of such security.
6. In case of shares and debentures, a certificate from a chartered accountant on the value of such securities according to the guidelines issued by SEBI or the erstwhile CCI for listed companies and unlisted companies, respectively.
7. Certificate from the concerned Indian company certifying that the proposed transfer of shares/convertible debentures by way of gift from resident to the non-resident shall not breach the applicable sectoral cap/FDI limit in the company and that the proposed number of shares/convertible debentures to be held by the non-resident transferee shall not exceed 5% of the paid-up capital of the company.

25 IMPORT OF CHEQUES, SECURITIES, CURRENCY & FOREIGN EXCHANGE

Checks

There are no restrictions on the import of foreign currency, checks, drafts, bills of exchange and any other financial instruments but the foreign exchange so received should be offered by the person receiving it for sale to an AD within seven days from the date of receipt.

Securities

There are no restrictions on the import (into India) of any security, whether Indian or foreign. It is, however, obligatory on the part of the persons resident in India (other than foreign nationals not permanently resident in India) to obtain RBI's permission to acquire or hold these securities.

Import of Indian Currency

No person is permitted to bring into India any Indian currency notes or coins except with the general or special permission of RBI. The conditions where import is permitted are:

(a) From Nepal by any person currency notes other than notes of the denominations of above Rs. 100;

(b) From other countries by Indian travelers currency notes of the government of India and RBI up to an amount not exceeding Rs. 5,000 per resident Indian, provided that the amount brought into India had earlier been taken out while proceeding abroad on a temporary visit.

Import of Foreign Exchange

Any person may bring foreign currency without limit into

India from any place provided that he declares it to the customs authorities on his arrival and declares the particulars of all such foreign currency brought in by him on the Currency Declaration Form (CDF). If the aggregate value of the foreign currency brought in currency notes, travelers checks, etc. does not exceed US$ 10,000 or its equivalent, and foreign currency notes do not exceed US$5000, CDF is not required to be completed.

Currency Declaration Form (CDF)

The CDF (if necessary) should be filled to avoid inconvenience at the time of departure.

CONCLUSION

I have enjoyed writing this book and it has been a great learning experience for me. The great benefit was that I have become aware of a myriad amount of information I would otherwise not have known.

I have, while writing on the rules as they pertain to non-residents, attempted to iterate that they must be aware of what they can and cannot do, and the things they should be careful about – how many days they can stay when they come to visit the country of their fathers, what they can and cannot bring, taxation and all other issues that affect the non-resident. Armed with the knowledge that I have tried to make them aware of through this book, they will be better able to handle their affairs in India.

I believe this book is crucial at this time considering the number of people emigrating to other countries and the number of people of Indian origin visiting India. Additionally, there are many returning for a time to India to work

My hope (as always) is that you, the reader - the NRI - will find this book as satisfying as I felt writing it. Only then will I believe that the purpose of writing this book has been accomplished.

APPENDIX A

FOREIGN EXCHANGE MANAGEMENT ACT (FEMA) AND FOREIGN EXCHANGE REGULATION ACT (FERA)

The difference between FERA and FEMA is not just a mere change of one word, from 'Regulation' to 'Management'. To understand the differences between the two statutes, we need to know the underlying principles that governed FERA. FERA was introduced at a time when forex reserves were very low. As such, it was believed that all foreign exchange earned by Indians rightfully belonged to the Government of India and had to be collected and relinquished to RBI promptly.

When FEMA was enacted on June 1, 2000, there was a general misunderstanding among NRIs that all restrictions and controls relating to foreign exchange transactions had been eliminated and that foreign exchange dealings would be allowed to be freely made after the introduction of FEMA. This is not so. It is, of course, true that there is a great change in the perspective of FEMA in comparison with FERA. But certain reasonable restrictions still exist in FEMA with regard to foreign exchange transactions so as to facilitate them in a regulated manner. Under FEMA, various notifications and provisions of the RBI Exchange Control Manual have been put together in the form of separate regulations for different types of exchange transactions with a view to making them available easily to NRIs and other persons, and to provide transparency to RBI rules and regulations. For example, the various types of accounts like NRE Account, FCNR Account, NRO Account, etc. were regulated through Exchange Control Manual and Notifications in this regard. Now, the FEMA (Deposit) Regulations deal with the maintenance and operation of such accounts in crystal clear manner. Similar is the case with reference to other various aspects of foreign exchange.

The primary change that the FEMA has brought in is that FEMA is a civil law, whereas the FERA was a criminal law. Under the FEMA no prosecution would be imposed for violation of operating provisions, likewise, arrest and imprisonment would not be resorted to except in the solitary case where the person, alleged to have violated the provisions of the FEMA, audaciously decides not to pay the penalty imposed under Section 13 of the FEMA. In the same manner unrestrained enormous powers of Directorate of Enforcement have been chopped down to a considerable extent. Even the word "offence" is conspicuous by its absence in the concrete provisions of FEMA.

The provisions of FERA were draconian in nature. These provisions empowered the Enforcement Directorate to arrest any person, search any premises, seize documents and start proceedings against any person for contravention of FERA or for preparations of contravention of FERA. The violation under FERA was treated as criminal offence and the burden of proof was on the guilty.

FEMA has reduced the austerity of exchange control by removing/mitigating the effect of these provisions. The contravention has been treated as civil offence. Primarily, for an offence, the accused cannot be arrested. He can be arrested only for non-payment of the penalty imposed for contravention. Specific provision has been made by fixing a time limit of twenty-four hours for bringing the arrested person before the Adjudicating Authority. Similarly, in respect of appeals filed before the Appellate Tribunal, a period of 180 days has been specified for final disposal of the appeals. No such time limit was laid down under FERA. The powers of Enforcement Directorate have been substantially reduced and new provisions for Adjudicating Authority and Compounding of cases have been introduced.

FEMA contains 49 sections in total. Of these, only seven sections, namely, Sections 3 to 9 deal with certain acts to be done or not to be done in connection with transactions involving foreign exchange, foreign security, etc. There are various sections from 16 to 35 relating only to adjudication and appeal. Further, one of the most important and distinguishing features of FEMA is that there is a provision for compounding of penalty as contained in Section 15 of FEMA, which was not available under FERA.

Whereas FERA contained 81 sections (some were deleted in the 1993 amendment of the Act) of which 32 sections related to operational part and the rest covered penal provisions, authority and powers of Enforcement Directorate, etc. Out of the 49 sections of FEMA, 12 sections cover operational part and the rest contravention, penalties, adjudication, appeals, enforcement directorate, etc. What was a full section under FERA seems to have been reduced to a sub-clause under FEMA in some cases.

For example,

(i) Section 13 of FERA provided for restrictions on import of foreign currency & foreign securities. Now this restriction is provided through a sub-clause 6(3) (g).

(ii) Section 25 of FERA provided for restrictions on Indian residents holding immovable properties outside India. Now the restriction is under sub-clause 6(4).

FERA regulated not just the foreign exchange transactions but also all financial transactions with non-residents. A FERA violation was treated as a crime. FERA primarily banned all transactions except those which were generally or specifically permitted by RBI. Whereas under FEMA, all current account transactions in forex like expenses that are not for capital purposes, are permitted except to that extent which is notified by the Central Government.

FEMA, 1999 contains only the concrete and procedural aspects of Foreign Exchange Regulations. The detailed provisions in regard to various aspects connected with Foreign Exchange Regulations are found in Rules, Regulations and Notifications under FEMA issued or disseminated by the Government of India or RBI. Thus, the Government of India, in exercise of the powers conferred on it under Section 46 of FEMA, has made various sets of Rules, namely-

1. Foreign Exchange Management (Current Transactions) Rules, 2000.
2. Foreign Exchange (Compounding Proceedings) Rules, 2000.
3. Foreign Exchange Management (Adjudication Proceedings and Appeal), Rules, 2000.
4. Foreign Exchange (Authentication of Documents) Rules, 2000.
5. Foreign Exchange Management (Encashment of Draft, Check Instrument and Payment of Interest) Rules, 2000.

The fundamental difference between FERA and FEMA is as under:

Under FERA, a normal operative section would provide that "no person can do the following transactions without general/special permission". Thus, for example, Section 9 prohibited all payments to non-residents. Then several notifications permitted payments subject to certain conditions. It meant that if there was no permission, a payment to a non-resident was prohibited.

Now under Section 5, all current account transactions are permitted under FEMA. RBI may regulate certain payments by issuing notifications/circulars. If there is a current account payment on which no notification has been issued, prima facie, it is permitted.

There is yet another major transformation in the protocol as far as regulation concerning immovable property situated in India is concerned. Under FERA acquisition of immovable property in India was governed by "citizenship criteria", whereas under FEMA the same is governed by "residential status" criteria. It means a foreign citizen who is resident in India (not being a citizen of any of the eight countries listed above) can purchase immovable property in India without any approval from RBI. He is also not required to file any declaration at the time of purchase of such immovable property.

Thus, FEMA has brought about a sea change in the hitherto difficult foreign exchange regulations. What was once considered draconian has been simplified largely for the benefit of non-residents thereby making their lives easier considerably.

APPENDIX B

SYNOPSIS OF FEMA REGULATIONS ON IMMOVABLE PROPERTY

Regulation 3

1. It deals with acquisition and transfer of immovable property in India by an Indian citizen resident outside India (NRI).
2. It grants general permission to him to acquire and transfer an immovable property in India other than agricultural land or plantation property or a farmhouse.

Regulation 4

1. It deals with acquisition and transfer of immovable property in India by a Person of Indian Origin (PIO).
2. It grants general permission to him to acquire and transfer (in certain situations) an immovable property in India other than agricultural land or plantation property or a farmhouse.

Regulation 5

It grants general permission to a person resident outside India who has secured RBI permission to establish a branch, office or other place of business in India (excluding a liaison office) to acquire an immovable property in India which is necessary for or incidental to carrying on the permitted activity.

Regulation 6

It deals with the repatriation of the sale proceeds by an NRI or a PIO, of an immovable property (other than agricultural land or plantation property or a farm house) in India subject to the satisfaction of certain stipulated conditions.

Regulation 7

It prohibits the acquisition or transfer of immovable property in India by citizens of certain neighboring countries, whether such an individual is a resident of India or not.

Regulation 8

It prohibits the transfer of an immovable property in India by a person resident outside India (other than an NRI or a PIO); i.e., a foreigner, without prior permission of RBI.

Thus, RBI has given only three 'General Permissions' (vide regulations 3, 4 and 5) in connection with immovable property in India to the following categories of Non-Residents:

1. A non-resident who is a citizen of India.
2. A non-resident who is a Person of Indian Origin (PIO).
3. A non-resident who has established in India a branch office or other place of business (excluding a liaison) office.

In all other cases, prior permission of RBI is required.